T0319201

Heritage Practices for Sustainability:
Ethnographic Insights from the BaTonga Community Museum in Zimbabwe

Munyaradzi Mawere

Langaa Research & Publishing CIG
Mankon, Bamenda

Publisher
Langaa RPCIG
Langaa Research & Publishing Common Initiative Group
P.O. Box 902 Mankon
Bamenda
North West Region
Cameroon
Langaagrp@gmail.com
www.langaa-rpcig.net

Distributed in and outside N. America by African Books Collective
orders@africanbookscollective.com
www.africanbookscollective.com

ISBN: 9956-763-07-1

© Munyaradzi Mawere 2016

Table of Contents

iv

Acknowledgements

This book is a development of my social anthropology mini-dissertation at the University of Cape Town (UCT) on heritage ethnography in rural Zimbabwe. My fieldwork in the Binga Community and the writing of this book involved the help of many people. However, there have been a select of few individuals whose intellectual contribution and support have led to this final product.

Firstly, I would like to express my heartfelt thanks to my supervisor, Professor Francis B. Nyamnjoh for your untiring guidance, acute insights and constructive criticism of my work as it progressed. Your criticism challenged my thinking to look at heritage issues with rigour and dexterity. I am similarly indebted to Professor Fiona Ross and the rest of the University of Cape Town's Anthropology section, who saw immediately the potential of this work and cheered me onward.

To those who helped me to gather data for my fieldwork, especially my research assistants, Joshua Chikozho, Alice Munkuli and Katekiso Konda, I have no words sufficient to express my profound and honest gratitude. You showed me all the necessary sign posts and richly endowed interlocutors to interact with during fieldwork. To my interlocutors, I say, the time spent becoming acquainted with all of you, your opinions, and intimate experiences enriched my perception of the world, and indeed my analysis of the material that make up this book.

I also wish to acknowledge my indebtedness to Mr and Mrs Bhondai for your generous hospitality, steadfast support and accommodating me on my way to and from my field site.

To my friends, siblings, and wife Annastacia, I wish to express my gratefulness for your unflagging support and encouragements. You never stopped believing in me, and your words of encouragement always inspired and emboldened me to work even harder than otherwise I might have done. Lastly, I thank the Almighty God for what you have made me to be, all that is, and all that is yet to materialise.

List of figures, tables and maps

List of Figures

List of Maps

List of Tables

Legal Instruments cited

Communal Lands Act of 1982
National Museums and Monuments Act chapter 25/11 of 1972
Provincial Councils and Administration Act Number 12
(Revised edition of 1996)
Rural District Council Act of 1998 (Revised edition of 1996)
Traditional Leaders Act Chapter 29: 17, Number 25 of 1998
The Constitution of Zimbabwe (2013)

List of Acronyms and Abbreviations

AD	In the Year of Our Lord
BBC	British Broadcasting Corporation
BCM	BaTonga Community Museum
BMLC	BaTonga Museum Local Committee
CCJPZ	Catholic Commission for Justice and Peace in Zimbabwe
CLA	Communal Lands Act
DA	District Administrator
GZNM	Great Zimbabwe National Monument
MP	Member of Parliament
NMMZ	National Museums and Monuments of Zimbabwe
PCAA	Provincial Councils and Administration Act
PF ZAPU	Patriotic Front- Zimbabwe African People's Union
RDCA	Rural District Councils Act
RDDC	Rural District Development Committee
TLA	Traditional Leaders Act
TRC	Truth and Reconciliation Commission
UCT	University of Cape Town
UNESCO	United Nations Educational, Scientific and Cultural Organisation
US$	United States Dollar
UZ	University of Zimbabwe
VIDCO	Village Development Committee
WADCO	Ward Development Committee
WHC	World Heritage Committee
WCED	World Commission on Environment and Development
ZANU (PF)	Zimbabwe African National Union – Patriotic Front

Chapter 1

Theory and Practice: Ethnographic Dissection through the Cultural Capital of the BaTonga People

What Theory is?

The term "theory" is a notorious notion that is difficult to pin down with precision. As such, there is no one universally accepted interpretation and definition of theory though there is a common ground and emphasis of recurring elements of what it entails. Due to this scenario, a wide array of definitions of theory has been conjured through time. Corrider (1985), for example, refers to theory as a coherent group of assumptions and propositions that can explain data. In more or less the same way, Jones (2000) understands theory as a formulation of the underlying principles of certain observations made on particular practical occurrences in a natural way and information about the observed occurrences is systematically organised and analysed over a reasonable period of time. A critical analysis of these definitions reveal that when talking of theory, we talk of a systematic organisation of generally accepted interdependent facts, principles, and assumptions of a given phenomenon particularly, on what happens, how and why it happens as such: it is an abstract idea testable in particular situations to determine its ability to achieve desired results i.e. its ability to understand, explain and interpret a given phenomenon. This means that in any theory, there are common positions that:

i). Theory involves abstraction;

ii). Theory also involves verifiable ideas, assumptions, formulations, propositions and organised facts;

iii). Theory helps us explain phenomenon.

Meshing theory and practice: Why theory matters for heritage studies?

In any discipline in the social sciences and humanities, theory matters. This is because there are certain occurrences in these disciplines that, for a long time, have been noted and some continue to be noted, yet people remain in the dark as what actually cause or influence such occurrences. The desire and thirsty to know, gather and verify the factors and causes of these occurrences, in this case those related to issues of heritage, in order to come up with compelling conclusions about the underlying influences of the occurrence yield what we call theory. Thus as soon as verifications of any given occurrence establish facts that can be generalised over an array of similar occurrences to explain how and why they occur, we already have a theory as our guide. This means that theory guide us in a number of ways so that we remain more focused and systematic in our thinking as we try to understand certain issues about a given phenomenon.

It should be underlined that the use of theory especially formulated from different backgrounds and contexts help us understand issues from different stand points. We cease from relying on a "single story" (Adichie 2009) but on multiple epistemological fronts. As Adichie tells us "the single story creates stereotypes, and the problem with stereotypes is not that they are untrue, but that they are incomplete." To avoid, the perpetuation of a single story, we need to apply critical theory in our interpretation of reality so as to accommodate multiplicities and diversity of perspectives of reality that more often than not are hidden to us by single stories. In other words, theory allows for "generative dialogue" (Verran 2011) whereby different theories are given the opportunity to speak to given data on different contexts or set-ups as they try to determine a deeper and nuanced understanding of a phenomenon. In the case of the BaTonga people, who are the subject for this book, more of a negative [single] story has been told since the colonial era through the present, resulting in the segregation of this minority group even in government policies.

Heritage in context: The BaTonga Community Museum

This research critically explores the socio-economic contribution and effects of cultural heritage sites on the livelihoods of local inhabitants of Binga –known as the BaTonga people – who live around the cultural heritage site of BaTonga Community Museum (henceforth referred to as BCM) in Zimbabwe. The BCM is one of the 17 registered national museums in Zimbabwe (Thondhlana 2015). It was established in 2000 but declared a national museum in September 2002. The museum is situated in Binga District, Matabeleland North Province, on the shores of Lake Kariba. It lies in the hot and arid Zambezi encampment, an area that was once a territory of tsetse fly. Because of its adjacency to Zimbabwe's major national tourist attraction, the Victoria Falls, coupled with cultural activities that are carried out at the BCM attracts a significant share of tourists both from within Zimbabwe and from abroad. Though a recently established cultural heritage site, this, among other reasons, makes the BCM one of the most important and promising cultural heritage sites in Zimbabwe.

Taking it from its French origin, the term 'heritage' is derived from *heriter* which means something passed on from an earlier generation to the next. This understanding of heritage relates it to history, which owes its origins from a Latin term *historia* meaning inquiry (Fisher 2010). However, David Lowenthal (1998) insists that history and heritage are two different worlds apart. He, in fact, argues:

History and heritage transmit different things to different audiences. History tells all who will listen what has happened and how things came to be as they are. Heritage passes on exclusive myths of origin and continuance,

3

endowing a select group with prestige and common purpose […] History is for all, heritage for (us) alone (p. 128-129).

Besides, heritage has been accused of being unscientific and an area that invests in emotions of, and allegiance to, imagined collective identities (Grever, De Bruijn and Van Boxtel 2012). Lowenthal (1996) captures this critique aptly when he argues that unlike history which is universally accessible and testable, heritage is "tribal, exclusive, patriotic, redemptive or self-aggrandising' and is not primarily concerned with 'checkable fact but credulous allegiance" (see, p. 120-121). Lowenthal goes on to argue that heritage embodies feelings of the past that shape identities and the historical materials that are harnessed to sustain them. For him, heritage's approach to the past is largely presentist and not particularly concerned with historical accuracy. Contrary to this approach is that of history, he argues further, which adheres to stipulated methods and ethics involving rigorous research, evidence, and rational arguments. In his comparison of heritage and history, Lowenthal (1998), thus argues:

Heritage diverges from history not in being biased but in its attitude towards bias. Neither enterprise is value-free. But while historians aim to reduce bias, heritage sanctions and strengthens it. Bias is a value that history struggles to exercise; for heritage, bias is a nurturing virtue (p. 122).

As Seixas (2014) has emphasised, the primacy of history is evidence not authority given that heritage tends to be celebratory while history critiques the past. In other words, heritage emphasises on the continuity from the past while history scrutinises and sometimes critiques or challenges the perceived links between the past and the present (Gadamer 1987).

I should point out, however, that even with all these seemingly incompatible divergences between heritage and history, it remains a fact that history and heritage converge, complement, and overlap. Both are, for example, approaches to the study of the past and their relationship as approaches is dialectical (Seixas 2014). More so, both heritage and history tend to be selective but strive to represent the totality and accuracy of the past (Lowenthal 1985). Moreover, heritage largely involves 'framing the past" and can become "as little more than bogus history' (Johnson 1999: 187) such that 'all that constitutes heritage enjoys the backing of history' (Tejaswi 2011: 1).

Though viewing history and heritage as separate practices, these overlaps prompted Lowenthal (1998) to identify some symbiotic relationships between them, particularly the manner in which heritage can be derived from historical narratives and the way in which heritage delivers history to the ordinary people. Lowenthal (1996: 250) argues:

> *Heritage experts* 'feel compelled to cloak (their) wares in historical authenticity. Material relics are scrutinised, memories retrieved, archives examined, monuments restored, re-enactments performed, and historic sites interpreted with painstaking precision. Heritage apes scholarship with factoids and footnotes' (p. 250).

What becomes evident from this discussion is that both heritage and history are approaches for the study of the past. They overlap and depend on each other in the sense that they derive their content about the past from each other. More importantly, both approaches are vulnerable to manipulation by various constituencies such as politics to address agendas of the time. As discussed later on in this thesis, the confusion on the relationship between heritage and history is conspicuously evident in the politics of heritage sites governance and management of Zimbabwe's cultural heritage sites such as museums.

Drawing it on its French etymology highlighted above, cultural heritage could be loosely understood as the physical (tangible) and non-physical (intangible) aspects of a particular

5

society normally inherited from past generations, maintained in the present and bestowed for the benefit of future generations. A cultural heritage can be natural – natural heritage – as in the case of culturally significant landscapes and biodiversity. Cultural heritage site is a place where the aspects of a cultural heritage are found, stored or displayed. Such sites include museums, shrines, temples, national archives, cultural centres, libraries, and commemorative and public spaces, among others (see for instance, Tanselle 1998; Hoffman 2006).

Many cultural heritage scholars have looked at heritage sites as centres for restoration of 'commemorative and public ceremonial places' (Rowlands 2008: 135), peaceful post-colonial order (Anderson 2006), cultural centres (Adorno 1983), and centres for appeasing while not confronting the past (Last 2000). This study draws on such related literature to examine the effects of heritage sites and their potentials as drivers for community development in Zimbabwe, with specific focus on the BCM. The questions explored in the study include:

- Who are the BaTonga people and what factors led to the establishment of their museum – the BCM?
- What could be the effect of such a cultural heritage site as the BCM on livelihoods of the local communities of Binga?
- What is the social relationship between humans, cultural objects and the state of rural livelihoods in Binga?
- How does the current governance of cultural heritage sites in Zimbabwe affect the conservation and socio-economic contributions of the sites?
- To what extent does community participation influence derivation of benefits from the BCM?
- What are the perceived effects of the BCM on the life-worlds and socio-economic development of the local community of Binga?
- What is the place of the BaTonga people in local thought regarding the protection and rehabilitation of the BCM?

6

In view of these questions, this study explores the agency of the BCM as a heritage site, and seeks to relate or even reconcile it with conceptions of nature, personhood and relationships of the local BaTonga people. This research further examines the potential of heritage sites to foster sustainable development of communities in which they are found. The study adopts BCM as its case study probing into the part being played by the museum in sustaining local livelihoods and promoting sustainable development. To ensure that a balance on the effects on local livelihoods of the BCM is attained, both negative and positive effects will be studied.

The rest of this introduction consists of the following parts: a) a condensed version explaining the distinction between effects and effectiveness as they relate to cultural heritage sites and people living around them; b) an outline of the research objectives and methodology; and c) an overview of the thesis structure and conclusion.

Cultural heritage sites and effects

The issue of effects and effectiveness in relation to cultural heritage sites is of critical importance in heritage studies. This section begins with clarification of the terms 'effects' and 'effectiveness' as understood and used in this study.

Effects in view of cultural heritage sites are different from effectiveness. One talks of effectiveness when intended objectives, actions or benefits are achieved, whereas effects are wider as they are usually more than just effectiveness. In other words, effectiveness addresses the extent to which conclusions could be determined by the context of a phenomenon, objective or action while effects (whether negative or positive) are normally measured either from the standpoint of the source, recipient or observer (Aslop and Tompsett 2007). As Denis Mcquail (1979) tells us, 'we can distinguish between effects and effectiveness, the former referring to consequences [...] whether intended or not, the latter to the capacity to achieve given objectives, whether this be attracting large audiences or influencing opinions and behaviour' (p. 8). Following Mcquail's explanation above, one could argue that effects do include unintended outcomes and could be in the medium or long term – they are often more difficult to measure using conventional methods that tend to focus on immediate or short term outcomes of an effective nature. On the other hand, as Halloran (1964) teaches us, effectiveness usually is determined by the source of a given phenomenon, agent, or act vis- a-vis those phenomena, agents or actions called upon to effectively bear the so-called 'effects' of the intentions of those who originate the communicative act.

While many heritage scholars have looked at various dimensions of cultural heritage sites, not many studies have specifically examined the effects and potential of cultural heritage sites as drivers for community development. Writing of Germany, Adorno, for example, is one among the first social theorists to see the importance of what he called the "culture industries" in which mass culture and communications are placed at the centre of leisure activity (see Adorno 1978; 1982; 1983; 1991). Examining the cultural institutions in contemporary societies of Germany such as the Frankfurt School, for example, Adorno argues that they stabilise capitalism and promote a consumer society based on homogeneous needs and desires for mass-produced products. This theorisation of the role of cultural institutions has, however, been criticised by scholars such as Walter Benjamin (1969) and Douglas Kellner (n.d) for its failure to accommodate oppositional practices and counter-hegemonic cultural strategies that promote diversity and multi-perspectival approach.

Whereas Adorno has talked of cultural institutions in Europe in terms of their roles, Rowlands (2008) has discussed restoration of cultural heritage sites such as public spaces and monuments in post-conflict situations in Africa focusing on Liberia. He observes that restoration of such sites as the National Museum of Liberia in the capital city of Monrovia, which was destroyed largely by a series of rocket attacks during a civil war in that country, is often associated with experiences and negotiations of reconciliation and trauma. Such restoration, Rowlands theorises, becomes possible only if people forget "absolutely" their troubled past. While forgetting allows restoration, revitalise unity of the nation and cultural heritage, and allows the re-emergence of a culture that sustains the continuity of an idea of civilisation and a move on with life, Rowlands is careful to note that it [forgetting] doesn't provide the opportunity for national grieving and public memorials. Taking a cue from Rowlands' analysis of memory, I add that forgetting the troubled past is likely to play down activities of healing, Truth and Reconciliation Commission (TRC) and results in future sprouts of violence between those that are perceived as perpetrators and victims of the past events. As Rowlands observes, forgetting also denies dignity, history, and 'voice to the victims' while robbing the society of conditions for social healing. Rowlands, thus, encourages 'forgetting in order to remember in a suitable way' as a better way for achieving restoration. On this note, he comments and accords credit to the physical rebuilding of the National Museum of Liberia and other such historic buildings after civil war.

Warnier, who has discussed heritage issues, including the human body, do so largely in terms of material culture (see Warnier 2001; 2005; 2007; Salpeteur and Warnier 2013). He considers material objects, for example the human body, as containers with inside and outside, openings and surfaces. For Warnier, besides such material objects being containers, they are actors in the material world that are constantly in a state of becoming given that by acting in a material world the object – or what he calls body 'supplements itself with innumerable surfaces and containers by means of which it extends beyond its own physical limits' (Warnier 2005: 186). However, Warnier as with Mauss (1950) and Berthelot (1995), finds it problematic to turn the body into anthropological object given that 'social and cultural facts are not the body in itself' but techniques of the

9

body. A technique is a 'traditional and efficacious action' (Mauss 1950: 371) on something which could be either a subject or object or both.

Warnier considers material culture as an essential component of the body or 'sensori-motoricity' as Warnier himself likes to call it. Material culture such as a museum – the BCM, for example – has an envelope and contents that like the museum itself is also a container. As such, material culture should be analysed and understood wholesomely through careful analysis of its contents, surfaces and even effects if one is to recognise it fully. This is because for Warnier, material culture in which containers, inside, outside, openings and surfaces could be found are all relevant in understanding the body and its conducts with other 'acting subjects.' Thus, Warnier understands 'bodily-and-material culture' as a system with consolidated entities and processes.

It is worth noting that although the abovementioned scholars do not specifically talk of agency of cultural heritage sites, their works imply that even cultural heritage sites as things have life. By tracing the effects of these cultural heritage sites, one can recognise their agency – their capacity as entities/"things," conscious or unconscious, to act or to mediate social relations. I should underline that agency is either unconscious and involuntary or purposeful and goal directed. This suggests that even cultural heritage sites are 'agentive entities' (Heath 2011) or what Warnier (2005) calls 'acting subjects', that is, 'subjects-acting- with-their-incorporated-objects' and sensori-affectivo motor conduct welded and mobilised together,' hence my argument in this study that even cultural heritage sites have agency that should be recognised. My argument here is germane to Schilder's (1964) insistence that *Körperschema* – bodily schema – does not end with its outside human skin as a limiting boundary. Instead, it extends far beyond the human skin to include all the objects that the body uses. It also includes all the material culture that lies beyond the body's immediate attention and grasp. The different cultural

10

artefacts in a museum, following Schilder, are incorporated into the bodily schema of the people who interact with the museum given that the objects are drawn from the larger environment in which both the museum and the people are part.

While tracing the effects of cultural heritage sites enables us to recognise what Heath calls 'non-human agency' – agency of things that are not considered as humans –, it also reconciles the effects with different conceptions of nature, personhood and relationships. On this note, this research further examines the potential of cultural heritage sites to promote development and sustain livelihoods of communities in which they are found. The study adopts the BCM examining the part being played by the museum in sustaining local livelihoods and fostering sustainable development. To ensure a balance on my analysis of the effects on local livelihoods of the BCM, both negative and positive effects are studied.

Research objectives

The main objective of this research is to establish, through ethnographic methods, the effects on local livelihoods of cultural heritage sites in Zimbabwe. Cultural heritage plays a significant role in both sustaining local livelihoods and promoting sustainable development in that it is an arena for identity formation and socio-economic growth (see for instance, Nurse 2006). As Nurse (2006) argues, culture is the fourth pillar of sustainable development along with social, economic and environmental dimensions. This implies that cultural heritage plays a significant role in both sustaining livelihoods and promoting socio-economic development. That said, the specific objectives of this research are:

i). To examine ethnographically and from the perspective of the locals the effects, both positive and negative, of cultural heritage sites and in particular the BCM in Zimbabwe as perceived and claimed by both the BaTonga and others.

11

ii). To examine factors that led to the establishment of the BCM.

iii). To explore the history of the BaTonga people and their BCM.

iv). To examine the effects of current governance and management of cultural heritage sites in Zimbabwe to the socio-economic contribution of the cultural heritage sites.

v). To examine whether the [local] epistemologies and environmental practices associated with activities at BCM in their complex everyday life make the museum a resource for promoting sustainability in Zimbabwe.

vi). To establish the status and contribution of BCM, in the local (in Zimbabwe nation-state) socio-economic development. This challenges the post-colonial Zimbabwean government's National Museums and Monuments of Zimbabwe (NMMZ) and scholars in Museology and Heritage studies for being silent on the effects and socio-economic potentials of BCM.

vii). To promote a 'generative dialogue' (Verran 2011) between contending approaches on the impact of cultural heritage sites in Zimbabwe. As Verran argues, such kind of dialogue opens possibilities for contending approaches to reach a compromise in order to achieve the best possible sustainable practices in the area.

Research methodology

This research was conducted in northwest Zimbabwe, particularly the BCM of Binga District in Matabeleland Province. Choice for this research area was premised on the fact that Binga is one of the under-researched areas in Zimbabwe. To gain access into the research site, traditional authority (chiefs and headmen) and government institutions involved in cultural heritage sites like NMMZ, who are custodians of culture and the environment, facilitated entry into the field site. These were useful in providing some important information on how sustainable livelihoods have been 'fostered' in the area over the years. Also, this was important to gain confidence of respondents, my security as the researcher, and dependability of results. Other support structures like print media and academic literature were ambassadors to data cases and other information relevant to this study.

For this study, ethnographic method of participant observation was the primary approach for gathering data. This method was appropriate for this study because 'it is both a humanistic method and a scientific one which produces the kind of experiential knowledge that allows one to talk convincingly' (Bernard 1995: 342) of a particular subject of study. This is not to say participant observation is without limitations. The researcher is aware that as an ethnographic method, participant observation requires the researcher to be flexible in responding to new ideas and methods should they become necessary. I [the researcher] was resident in my field site – BCM in Binga – for a period of about one month (between July and August 2015). As one familiar with the Shona language (one of the two languages widely spoken in Binga), I was able to participate in most of their daily interactions, of course, not all of them. During the time I was carrying out fieldwork in Binga, I interacted with a number of interlocutors on one-on-one basis and through focus group discussions, including visitors (local and international) to the BCM. Table 1 below shows the number of people I interacted with during fieldwork:

It should be acknowledged that I could not interact with all the members in Binga as it is often difficult to do so when carrying out fieldwork. In fact the best way when carrying out research is to come up with a sample based on the representation of the whole population through both purposeful and/or snowball sampling. Purposeful sampling was used for traditional leaders, NMMZ employees, and village elders, who I believed were key stakeholders and custodians of cultural heritage in the area.

Table 1: Demographic profile of people I interacted with during fieldwork

Designation	Female	Male
NMMZ	2	5
Traditional Leaders	1	3
Village Elders	9	9
Local Youths	12	12
Craft Centre Members	5	5
University Students	1	1
Visitors	6	9
Total	**36**	**44**

As Breen (2007) argued, stakeholders in cultural heritage are community elders and community members because elders are custodians of traditions and pass them on and interpret them whenever there is a dispute and community members are to uphold and preserve traditions. Snowball was used for the other group members who participated in this study to determine people who were critical in my study and as such I was informed by my research assistants that they had the best knowledge required in the area of study. Besides, the participants derived benefits from the cultural heritage site and represented the whole community such that it could be argued that the research methodology I adopted is justifiable as it involves both stakeholders and key respondents in this study.

With the consent of my interlocutors, I also listened to stories, observed, kept a field diary of interactions/field notes, and video recorded 'naturally' occurring communicative interactions with the participants in a range of everyday life activities. Stories (though they might be fiction), for example, 'succeed in giving us a vivid sense of what is at stake at any moment of being, and in introducing us to some of the ways in which existential-phenomenological thought has theorised the question of being' (Jackson 2005: xiii).

To facilitate access to the community members and to ensure that data collection occurred from multiple perspectives, three key research assistants from within the community where field work was carried out were selected on voluntary basis. Multiple observations have the merit that they allow for patterns to be identified so that verification of data can be done before it is presented. The research assistants also assisted me with data collection; provided additional observations and information on the social meanings and significance of some local practices. Besides, the research assistants helped in conducting structured and semi structured in-depth interviews, group focus discussions, informal conversations and observations. Interviews, discussions and observations focused on the locals' beliefs, forms of livelihoods, their symbolic significance of different daily practices, their views of the BCM and aspirations as a people.

As gathered data consisted of recordings of natural communicative interactions that demonstrated the rural communities' life histories, underlying beliefs, livelihood sources, relations and interactions with the "natural" environment on daily basis, I drew from analytical approach of 'social interaction analysis' (Kendon 1990) and discourse analysis (Fairclough 1989) of all forms of relations between the locals – the BaTonga people, the BCM, and the "natural" environment in general.

The journey through the book

In this last section, I briefly outline the structure of the book.

Chapter two of this book discusses research background and literature while providing the theoretical framing for the book. I introduce and elaborate upon Kopytoff's cultural biographical approach. I recognise Kopytoff's work is not without its faults and therefore I seek to enhance it by drawing upon other theoretical works to articulate what I call a "critical Kopytoffian perspective".

Chapter three provides context for my specific study by examining the experiences of the BaTonga people of Binga (both before and after the construction of Kariba Dam) and showing the continuing agency and relevance of culture to the post-Kariba Dam era. More specifically, I go on to consider culture as it is embedded in the philosophy of life of the BaTonga people. This assists in locating my study of the effects of cultural heritage sites on local livelihoods in Binga District contemporary Zimbabwe.

Chapter four provides a general overview of the research findings by addressing questions of effects and effectiveness as articulated by community members (or research participants) and giving a sense of the commonalities and differences between responses by the research participants.

Chapter five addresses more particular themes about effects of the BCM. It shows the complexity of distinguishing effects and effectiveness and nuanced character of cultural heritage sites and the fact that these sites are always in the process of becoming as community members around the sites and visitors alike try to make sense of the world around them.

Finally, in chapter six, I provide a synthetic and coherent overview of (and conclusion to) the thesis by integrating the theory and evidence on the effects of cultural heritage sites as discussed in previous chapters. It also underlines the contribution of the thesis to existing knowledge in cultural heritage studies in the light of critical Kopytoffian perspective adopted and the ways in which this perspective can be enhanced.

Conclusion

This introductory chapter has articulated the main objective (as well as specific ones) and focus of this book – that of exploring the socio-economic contribution and effects of the BCM to the local BaTonga people.

The chapter has disentangled central concepts that run throughout the study such as culture heritage, effects, effectiveness, and agency, among others. This has been done upfront to ensure an easy following of the discussion by the reader.

The chapter has spelt out the methodology used to conduct the research that culminated into this book, before outlining the structure of the book. In the next chapter, I focus on literature review and background to the study.

18

Chapter 2

Merging Theory and Practice in Heritage Studies:
A Critical Review

The BaTonga Community Museum

The BCM is situated in the Binga District of northern Zimbabwe. This is one of the most 'remote' areas of Zimbabwe; an area which through its numerous markets selling wooden crafts and other such handicrafts like baskets and mats evoke and demonstrate the pervasiveness of ethnic branding – 'ethnicity' (Comaroff and Comaroff 1993; 2009; 2012) in Zimbabwe. Ethnicity is understood in this study as a loose, labile repertoire of signs by means of which relations are constructed and communicated through which a collective consciousness of cultural likeness is rendered sensible (Comaroff and Comaroff 1993). It is a shared expression, through tangible, marketable, owned products, symbols, and practices that signify individual and group *essence* of a people (in this case the BaTonga people) with a common history. This means that ethnicity as a process has enormous potential either to 'improve' or 'destruct' socio-economic relationships in a given society.

I should underline that Binga District has been marginalised since the colonial period in Zimbabwe. By marginalisation (which is also known as social exclusion), I mean social disadvantage and relegation of individuals or the entire community to the periphery of the society socially, politically, economically and culturally (see also Silver 1994). As Lewis and Lockheed (2006: 49) argue, 'marginalisation sidelines certain population groups. It *restricts* excluded groups' economic mobility and *prevents* them from receiving the social rights and protections meant to be extended to all citizens.' This means that marginalisation has, as its effects, some individuals or the entire community of some people being systematically blocked, partially or totally, from accessing various resources, opportunities, and rights that are normally accessible to other members of a different group of the same society. The denial of access through marginalisation normally results in livelihoods insecurity and consequently poverty of the excluded group as they fail to realise their full potential (cf. British Broadcasting Corporation [BBC] News 2006). It also consolidates ethnic differences and tribalism in some cases.

During the colonial era, Binga District was marginalised and made to lag behind in terms of economic development for the major reason that it was tsetse-fly infested and drought-prone as it is located in Zimbabwe's agro-zone region 5, a region with poor annual rainfall. Zimbabwe is divided into five agro-ecological regions known as natural regions. The division, which was effected in the 1960s, is mainly based on the annual amount of rainfall received, soil quality and vegetation type, with the declining of the quality of the land resource declining from Natural Region 1 through to Natural region 5 (Moyo 2000). While the agro-zone region 1 has low temperatures, high altitude of about 1500m, and receives an annual average of 1000 mm, most of which falls throughout the year, region 5 covers the lowland areas below 900m above sea level and receives highly erratic annual average amount of less than 650 mm (Ibid; Rukuni and Eicher 1994). Region 5 is in fact, unsuitable for crop production but for extensive livestock and game-ranching. Yet, although regions 5 (and 4) are too dry for crop production, people in these regions also grow grain crops such as maize and millet as well as cash crops like cotton for their food security. Maps 1, 2 and 3 below show the location of Binga District, Binga District Map, and the 5 Natural (Agro-ecological) Regions of Zimbabwe respectively.

Map 1: Location of Binga District in Zimbabwe

Source: Surveyor General (1984)

Map 2: Binga District Map

Source: BaTonga Community Museum

Map 3: Natural (Agro-ecological) regions of Zimbabwe

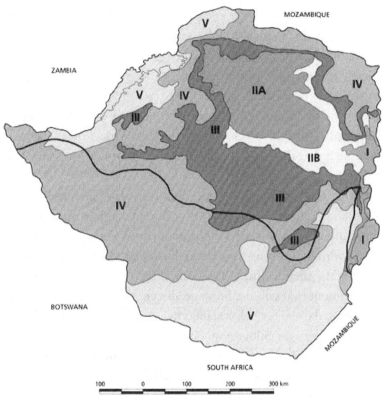

Source: Surveyor General (1984)

The area around Binga District has remained marginalised even after Zimbabwe political independence in 1980 mainly because of the BaTonga people's closeness to the Ndebele ethnic group in the same Matabeleland Province, a group that for the larger part of the pre-colonial era and the early years of national independence of Zimbabwe (before the 1987 Unity Accord between Zimbabwe African National Union Patriotic Front (ZANU-PF) and Patriotic Front Zimbabwe African People's Union (PF ZAPU) was in direct conflict with Zimbabwe's biggest ethnic group, the Shona who have happened to be at the helm of the government since the country's independence. Due to ethnic differences which resulted in the 1980-87 political instability and the atrocities duped *gukurahundi*–literary mean the early rain which washes away the chaff before the spring rains – which had the effect of causing more than 20, 000 civilian deaths (CCJPZ 1999; Makambe 1990). The continued marginalisation of the BaTonga people means their agency as a people as well as their collective expression has been negatively impacted upon by the political and socio-economic environment in Zimbabwe. The situation obtained during and after colonialism, thus, clearly demonstrated the need for the BaTonga people to reclaim their collective history, identity, and culture.

The establishment of the BCM by the government of Zimbabwe through its NMM – the managing authority of museums and monuments in the country –was a gesture towards empowering the long neglected BaTonga communities while promoting their culture. This was after the realisation by the government that cultural heritage all over the world is becoming an essential drive for cultural identity, sustainable livelihoods and development. As Silberberg (1995) tells us, there has been a clarion call all over the world for communities living near cultural heritage sites to use their cultural heritage to stimulate sustainable development. For Silberberg, the call is important because cultural heritage and sustainability are intimately linked. Besides, the goals of sustainable development are to continuously assist cultural heritage conservation in development projects for communities thereby ensuring the process heritage conservation and maintenance of cultural identities among nation-states. On this note, credit should be accorded to the Bruntland Commission of 1987 which proposed a working definition for sustainable development that has become a yardstick for many nations today. Bruntland defined sustainable development as a 'development that meets present needs without compromising the ability of future generations to meet their own needs' (WCED 1987:43).

Since the Bruntland Convention in 1987, cultural heritage sites across the world have been perceived as an economic

24

necessity and a public requirement with symbolic value and measurable benefits (Breen 2007). The stakeholders in cultural heritage include community elders, community members, visitors, and the government. Amongst the stakeholders, elders are possibly the greatest custodians of culture and traditions with the duty to protect and pass them on to next generations and interpret them to visitors or whenever a dispute arises. No wonder scholars like Harrison *et al* (2010) and Eboreime (2009) argue that cultural heritage offers considerable opportunities for community empowerment through its potential to mobilise resources for cultural tourism and crafts; and should be continuously negotiated and renegotiated in order to meet the demands of the present generation without compromising that of the future generations as a means of survival.

Zimbabwe is blessed with many places with cultural and/or national significance, some of which have been placed in the United Nations Educational, Scientific and Cultural Organisation (UNESCO) list of World Heritage Sites. The cultural heritage sites – cultural properties of outstanding universal value – in Zimbabwe include but not limited to Great Zimbabwe National Monument, Khami National Monument, Matobo Cultural Landscape, Domboshava National Monument, and the BaTonga Community Museum. These sites should be windows to sustainability of livelihoods and development of the communities living in their vicinity. The Zimbabwean nation-state has since realised the role that heritage sites are playing in improving development and the lives of local community members. In its first five year development plan of 1986-90, Zimbabwe through its arm, the ZNMM, indicated that monuments such as Great Zimbabwe were well marked for tourism which could possibly and effectively impact positively on the national economy. The objective of the government of Zimbabwe, through the aforementioned plan, was to ensure that development of monuments and museums as tourist assets should result in the creation of new employment opportunities and raise the standard of living of the people living in the rural areas (Collett 1988:5). It is in the light of these developments that the BCM was established in 2000.

Interrogating heritage literature

The study of cultural heritage sites in Zimbabwe, as elsewhere in the world, is not new in scholarship. Beyond Zimbabwe, most of the scholars who have studied cultural heritage have looked at cultural heritage sites as centres for restoration of 'commemorative and public ceremonial places' (Rowlands 2008: 135; 1993; 1985), peaceful post-colonial order (Anderson 2006), cultural centres (Adorno 1983), and centres for appeasing while not confronting the past (Last 2000).

In Zimbabwe, scholars who have studied celebrated cultural heritage sites have concentrated largely on the history and politics (see Ranger 1999; Fontein 2006), management (see Matenga 1998; Ndoro 2001a, b), legislation, conservation, and preservation (see Taruvinga and Ndoro 2003; Pwiti 1996; Pwiti and Chirikure 2008; Pwiti and Mvenge 1996) of heritage sites such as Great Zimbabwe National Monuments (GZNM). The effects of cultural heritage sites on local livelihoods and sustainable development are yet to receive serious attention from scholars and researchers. By livelihood, I mean an integrative term that include activities, entitlements, and assets by which people do make a living through natural or biological means (i.e. land, water, common property resources, flora and fauna), social or cultural means (i.e. community, family, social methods, participation and empowerment) and/or human means (i.e. knowledge and skills) (Carney 1998; Mawere 2013; Bebbington 1999). A livelihood is sustainable 'if it can cope with, and recover from stresses and shocks, and can maintain or enhance its capabilities and assets both now and in the future while not undermining the resource base' (Campbell and Luckert 2002: 14). This entails that livelihoods can only be sustainable – what can be termed sustainable development – if and only if they can help to improve lives of the people now and

26

without compromising lives of future generations. As highlighted above, there is dearth of literature that specifically and explicitly examines the effects on local livelihoods of heritage sites in view of socio-economic development and sustainability especially in Zimbabwe where specific reference for this study is made.

In addition to the above, it is generally agreed that sustainability of cultural heritage is much more difficult as compared to that of natural heritage (see Kiriama *et al.* 2010; Moscardo 2001; Faulkner *et al.* 2001). Kiriama *et al* (2010:4), for instance, argues that sustainable development models are quite difficult to apply when it comes to cultural heritage since it is a non-renewable resource. Yet, there is dearth of literature that aim at investigating the validity of Kiriama *et al*'s assertion. In view of this realisation and the main objective of this thesis, the present study partly investigates Kiriama *et al*'s assertion by assessing the extent to which cultural heritage, and in particular the BCM, has and continue to contribute to socio-economic development of local communities.

In Zimbabwe, this has been aggravated by the point that a considerable number of researches that have been carried out on cultural heritage sites have concentrated more on big heritage sites such as GZNM, Khami Ruins, and Matopos (see for example Garlake 1975, 1982; Fontein 2006; Pwiti 1996; Ranger 1999). Great Zimbabwe National Monument, for instance, being the most popular tourist destination in the country after Victoria Falls, has over the years enjoyed studies by scholars across disciplines. Smaller and recently established heritage sites have received little attention from researchers. In the case of the BCM, three major reasons have resulted in the site receiving insignificant attention from scholars. These are: First, the BCM is situated in one of the most remote and marginalised areas of Zimbabwe where accessibility is difficult. Second, the BCM is a relatively 'young' heritage site only established in the 21st century, and in particular 2000. As such, the BCM is still yet to receive adequate attention from scholars and researchers. Third, most

27

of the researchers on Zimbabwe's cultural heritage sites seem to be more interested in the most popular heritage sites such as GZNM.

The above cited observation is true when looking at the number of researches and literature that has been generated over the years on GZNM. The anthropologist, Joost Fontein (2006) in: *The silence of Great Zimbabwe: Contested landscapes and the power of heritage*, for example, have studied the historical and political contestations associated with Great Zimbabwe National Monument which happens to be the biggest national monument in Zimbabwe. Basing on his findings, Fontein describes GZNM as a centre of contest and controversy between 'professional' archaeologists, 'amateur' Rhodesian 'antiquarians' and people living around the site over who should be accorded the authority to interpret and overseer the welfare of the site. Terence Ranger (1999) in his *Voices from the rocks*..., also looks at aesthetic nature, religious significance, culture and history of another popular cultural heritage site in Zimbabwe known as Matopos Hills in north-western part of the country. Pwiti and Mvenge (1996) examine problems associated with the management of rock art sites in Zimbabwe particularly at Domboshava National Monument. Chiwaura and Chabata (2014) have looked at the contestations associated with tangible and intangible values of heritage in view of another famous cultural heritage site in Zimbabwe known as Chitungwiza chaChaminuka Shrine. Other scholars who have studied cultural heritage sites in Zimbabwe have examined different aspects of the Great Zimbabwe Monument, ranging from its history (see Garlake 1975, 1982; Ranger 1999), culture (see Matenga 1998), and management (see Ndoro 2001a, b, 2005), and religious significance, contestations and interpretation (see Mawere, Sagiya and Mubaya 2013). Thus, most of the studies on cultural heritage sites in Zimbabwe concentrate on popular heritage sites in the country besides excluding the aspects of effects of heritage sites on the communities where they are found.

To unravel the nuances and subtleties around Zimbabwe's cultural heritage sites, this study examines the effects of the BCM to the people living in the vicinity of the site. Unpacking the effects of cultural heritage sites in Zimbabwe is useful in rethinking social networks and strategies for sustainable development in the country and more specifically in view of the BaTonga people. This work thus brings epistemological 'defamiliarisation' (Shklovsky 1917 cited in Crawford 1984) as it questions the familiar. In Anthropological theory, questioning the familiar is important as it allows us to understand the deep structural tensions/contradictions in knowledge and open up new epistemic positions. Thus, this work quests to expose to the twilight zone the different angles from which cultural heritage sites could affect [positively or otherwise] locals in Zimbabwe; to examine how locally generated knowledge could be legitimised and harnessed for both the human and environmental good; to foster 'ethno-science' (Altieri 1995); and to deploy in practice 'symmetrical anthropology' (Latour 1993, 2007) – a novel anthropology that practically moves beyond the nature/culture divide and is open-ended; and to justify and bring into Zimbabwean education system the cultural heritage conservational practices of the locals, thereby closing the theoretical and practical research gaps highlighted above.

In view of the abovementioned gaps and shortcomings, the study adopts as its theoretical framework a cultural biographical approach (Kopytoff 1982, 1986; Kopytoff and Miers 1977) – an approach of studying cultures that allows the analysis of relationships between persons and things as a process of social transformation that involves a series of changes in status. As Kopytoff (1986) insists, cultural biographical approach is culturally informed given that things are culturally constructed in much the same way people are culturally constructed: things take part in a culture, constructed and reconstructed through time. I add that though Kopytoff does not explicitly argue that things have life, his cultural biographical approach implies this and that by tracing a biography of a thing we recognise its agency as well. In fact, the emergent field of material culture studies has underscored the extent to which objects just like persons lead social lives as they interact with humans or amongst themselves, hence have agency which enable them to transgress the usual boundaries between them and persons. This resonates with Appadurai's discussion of social life of things. Elaborating on the "social life of things," Appadurai (1986) has made an attempt to transgress the conceptual dichotomy between subjects and objects. Similarly but using cultural biographical approach, this study seeks to argue for the rethinking of strategies for interacting with cultural heritage sites by locals – the BaTonga people of Binga; to argue that cultural heritage sites conservation using the principles of expert science alone should be reconsidered and reinterpreted from a post-humanities approach that appreciates all possible dimensions and promotes human-other beings sustainable interactions as best possible environment conservation and cultural heritage sites management practices. The present study, however, goes beyond Kopytoff (1986) to explicitly argue that things have life, what Appadurai refers to as the 'social life of things.' Taking into account Alfred Gell's (1998) provocative analysis of art and agency, the study critically examines 'a domain in which 'objects' merge with 'people' by virtue of the existence of social relations between persons and things, and persons and persons *via* things' (p. 12). In this regard, this study argues for a critical cultural biographical approach – what I call critical Kopytoffian perspective in this study– that is, a perspective that takes into account agency of things and in particular how "things" mediate social agency between and amongst themselves. This kind of approach is echoed by Jakob von Uexkull (2010) who encourages us (human beings) to 'think' from the perspective of animals (in the case of my research, to think of effects and socio-economic contribution of cultural heritage sites from the perspective of the locals – the BaTonga people of Binga together with their immediate environment). This approach, which seriously consider the other (whether humans or things), is germane to the one that Wim van Binsbergen (2003) emphasises in his notion of intercultural inquiry/philosophy as a methodology to explore with informants' (or interlocutors[1]) communicative actions and questions on their understandings on the nature of existence of things. In the words of van Binsbergen: 'Ethnographers can only claim credibility provided that, in their fieldwork and in the production of published texts, ample provision has been made to turn their ethnography into a form of 'communicative action' (p. 504). This is very similar to the anthropological approach that Lien and Law (2010: 5) allude to when they argue that 'through attention to practices and performativity, we may contribute to an anthropology which is more sensitive to relations between humans and other living beings than is possible in a more anthropocentric approach'. Lack of a 'sustainable dialogue' between humans, state, forests and cultural heritage sites seems to have been prompted by the idea that humans are superior to nature. This has been noted by Fairbanks (2010: 8) who avers: 'Until recently, Western virtue ethics has never recognised nature-focused virtues. This is not surprising, since Western philosophies and religions have promoted the ideas that humans are superior to nature and that there are no moral principles regulating our relationship to nature'. Yet 'this anthropocentric approach emphasises particular qualities of the human-animal phenomena on the basis of relations of asymmetry marked by animal subordination. In other words, it separates "culture" (human) and "nature" (non-

---

[1] In this study, the concepts "informant" and "interlocutor" are used interchangeably to refer to research participants. However, the word "interlocutor" is preferred, as in Zimbabwe, especially during the liberation struggle, "informant" was a loaded term used to refer to traitors [vatengesi] who collaborated with the colonial enemy (Muzvidziwa 2004: 305; Mawere 2015). Besides, the concept of "interlocutor" better reflects the exchange of ideas, collaborations, interactions and negotiations that normally take place between the ethnographer (or anthropologist) and research participants during research, and indeed the production of particular kinds of knowledge. No wonder Devisch (in Devisch and Nyamnjoh 2011, 16) refers to the relationship between an anthropologist and interlocutor (research participant) as ideally one of "mutually enriching co-implication."

31

human) on the basis of unequal distribution of agency' (Lien and Law 2010:10). This binary has the disadvantage and [negative] effect of upsetting the natural ecosystem as it gives humans the mandate to exploit nature without recourse.

Conclusion

Recent studies on cultural heritage sites in Zimbabwe and elsewhere have concentrated more on celebrated cultural heritage sites, heritage management, legislation, conservation, and preservation. As already discussed in this chapter, a lot has been written on cultural heritage sites in Zimbabwe and beyond. Yet, it remains a great surprise that the effects of heritage sites on local livelihoods and sustainability especially in relation to small and relatively newly established heritage sites haven't received staid attention from scholars and researchers. There is insignificant attention by many cultural heritage researches when it comes to the study of the effects on local livelihoods of cultural heritage sites and their current governance in view of socio-economic development and sustainability especially in Zimbabwe where specific reference for this study is made.

Besides, while it is generally agreed that sustainability of cultural heritage is much more difficult as compared to that of natural heritage, there is dearth of literature that aim at investigating the validity of this assertion. In view of this realisation and the main objective of this thesis, the present study partly aims to investigate this assertion by assessing the extent to which cultural heritage, and in particular the BCM, has and continue to contribute to socio-economic development of local communities. In the light of the aforementioned gaps, the present study, thus, makes an attempt to examine the socio-economic and effects on local livelihoods of the BCM.

The next chapter provides context for my specific study by examining the experiences of the BaTonga people of Binga (before, during, and after the construction of Kariba Dam). In that attempt, the chapter shows the effects, agency, governance politics of cultural heritage sites in Zimbabwe, and the continued relevance of culture to the contemporary BaTonga people.

Chapter 3

Entering the Field Site:
Imbibing from the BaTonga Wellsprings of Knowledge

Introduction

It was on a Saturday on 11 July, 2015 that I arrived at my fieldwork site, the BaTonga Community Museum (BCM), to start my ethnographic fieldwork in Matabeleland Province, northwestern Zimbabwe. I had already talked to Mr Joshua Chikozho, the Curator-in-charge of the BCM, where I would reside for the next thirty days while doing fieldwork in the area. Joshua is the friend of a friend at Great Zimbabwe University. He has been with the museum for twelve years, since 2004, and was quite familiar with the local language, people, and the geography of the area itself. Joshua readily agreed to be one of my research assistants, and to share accommodation with me at his museum premises.

On Friday 10 July 2015, I boarded the bus to my fieldwork site. The journey was too long, some 600 km away, so I had to sleep over in Bulawayo before I proceeded the next day. I had arranged with Joshua's in-law, Mr Bhondai that I sleep-over at his house for a night. On the following morning, Mr Bhondai took me to the bus terminus where I had to board the bus to Binga Business Centre, my actual destination where the BCM is located. I got the first bus which usually leaves the bus terminus at 6 O'clock in the morning to reach the Binga Business Centre at around 3 O'clock in the afternoon. I chose the front seat so that I could have a full view of the scenery outside as we travelled. Since it was the July Winter season, the vegetation on both sides of the road was dry that through the window I could observe the vegetation and homesteads a distance away from the road. I observed that the road was very winding and with many pot holes, curves and rugged terrain in some parts. I was afraid we would be involved in an accident before I reach my destination. It was a tarred road which made it easier for the driver to negotiate curves and to speed up where clear.

We drove past a valley area with a vast thick forest on both sides of the road. At bus stops along the road, I could also see woven baskets, curved artefacts, and earthenware pots on display. Beyond, some round houses on stilts could be seen. I appreciated the beauty of the artefacts and houses. From a distance the houses I saw appeared unique and beautifully constructed. "How do people make these beautifully designed things!" I said to myself. My ethnographic fieldwork had started.

At 2: 50 pm I arrived at Binga Business Centre. Joshua was already waiting for me in his car parked at the bus terminus. He welcomed and immediately allocated me a room in a house I had to share with him and his family for the next one month of my study. See figure 1 below shows the house I was resident during my fieldwork in Binga.

Figure 1: House where I was resident during fieldwork

Early the next morning, Joshua and I set out for our tour around Binga Communal Area. Since it was on a Sunday, he was available to take me around the villages in the area. Initially, I was a bit unease. I was not sure I would be able to communicate efficiently in Tonga language (known as Chitonga) which is different from Shona – the language I am conversant with and speak efficiently – but was happy when I realised Joshua was very fluent in Chitonga. Also, I realised that most of the people we met as we toured the area were fluent in both Chitonga and Shona languages. So, I would communicate with the language I am most familiar with. Besides, all the people we met along the way and in the villages welcomed us as they knew Joshua very well. Of particular interest was meeting Mr Katekiso Konda (not his real name) and his wife, a very cheerful and hospitable couple. Katekiso was a good friend of Joshua, and had known each other for some time. After my research assistant – Joshua – introduced me to the couple, Mrs Konda started preparing us some breakfast while we were talking to her husband. I did not want to have the breakfast but Joshua reminded me that it was contrary to the philosophy of Ubuntu – a philosophy of humanness that emphasises respect, oneness, unity and sharing. In fact it was considered bad manners to refuse food in the village, especially from a good friend like Katekiso. So, we had our breakfast together as we continued our conversation with Katekiso, in which I learnt that he and his wife were born and raised in Binga. I also learnt that Katekiso was an accomplished wood carver/carpenter and his wife an accomplished basket maker. Certainly, the couple had vast experiences and knowledge about wood curving and basketry. They showed us some of the objects they make. The objects were wonderfully done. With the couple's consent, I took photos of some of the objects. I also asked if Katekiso was available to be my second research assistant, and he agreed. Given that he was not formerly employed, he would take me around the villages during weekdays when Joshua was at work. We talked for about three hours before we dearly thanked Katekiso and his wife for their hospitality and bade farewell.

Joshua and I continued with our tour around the village. I could observe the unmistakable unique BaTonga culture architecture commonly described as houses on stilts *(Ngazi* in Chitonga*)* at close range. As Joshua and many other people we met testified, these houses have become one of the pillars of the BaTonga culture and identity. The houses, which are beautifully built, are normally raised about six feet or so above the ground surface. Although the *Ngazi* itself is circular, the platform on which it stands is often projected to provide a rectangular verandah. Mopane (*Colophospermum mopane*) is normally used for support poles given that it is a hardwood particularly good for house frames and resistant to attacks by both wood beetle and white ant. The architecture bears testimony to the enduring self-belief spirit, resourcefulness and genius creativity of the BaTonga people. See figure 2 below which shows *Ngazi* of the BaTonga people:

Figure 2: Houses on stilts known as *Ngazi*

The interplay of the natural and cultural resources I witnessed through observations of socio-cultural objects of the BaTonga people shows a people in charge of their lives, culture, and identity. Clearly, the architecture of the BaTonga people is different from most of the architecture found elsewhere in Zimbabwe. When I asked why the BaTonga built houses on tilts, which are quite different from those in many other parts of Zimbabwe, three reasons were given. The first was: Long ago the area covering Binga Communal Area had many predators such as lions, leopards, snakes, and hyenas, so people saw it safer to sleep in raised houses than those built at ground level. The second one was: Binga is one of the hottest areas in Zimbabwe. Thus, going by the scientific law of 'the higher you go the cooler it becomes,' the BaTonga wanted to enjoy cool weathers. Thirdly, it was reported that Binga Communal Area being located in a valley, sometimes people suffer from floods. Building the houses on raised ground, therefore, would make the BaTonga people safer during flood periods. These three observations I made resonate with Reynolds' observation that each housing architectural form is a well-balanced solution to the problem of living in a particular climate, environment and society (Reynolds 1986).

I was very happy about having made such a good start which I never imagined before. We followed the small winding paths in the bush and in between village homesteads. As we walked, we could hear the sounds of singing birds from all sides. We did not visit BCM as Joshua had promised to take me there the following day, Monday. At around 3: 30 pm, we headed back to our residence.

The next day, Joshua took me to the BCM for a tour in the museum. He introduced me to all the workers at the museum including Alice, his secretary and a female tour guide at the museum. Alice was in her mid-twenties. She was a humorous, open-minded, and seemingly an intellectually gifted woman. After the introductions and a conversation with Alice for a couple of minutes, I kindly asked if she could be available as my third research assistant. I wanted her to assist me gathering data about the women life-worlds that might be difficult for me as a male researcher to gather on my own. Alice took me around the museum, the Crafts and Art Centre located about 5m from the museum, and the library, showing me all the different objects stored therein. In the museum, Alice would explain all bits about the function or purpose of each and every object we encountered. Gifted in humour and well-grounded in the history and culture of the BaTonga people, she would also cheerfully and splendidly answer to all the questions I posed about the objects in the museum and the culture of the BaTonga people.

Setting the BaTonga People and the BaTonga Community Museum in history

According to history, the BaTonga people, now the inhabitants of one of the remotest parts of northwestern Zimbabwe, particularly Binga District, Matabeleland Province, trace their origins back to central Africa. They are believed to have arrived in northwestern Zimbabwe about AD 300 (see for instance, Reynolds 1989). In Zimbabwe, the BaTonga people number up to 5000,000 and are mostly subsistence farmers who speak a language called Chitonga (Kwekudee 2014). Their forefathers favoured the riverine areas along the Zambezi, Kana, Mzola and Tshongokwe Rivers in Zimbabwe and Zambia where they cultivated alluvial soils based on recession agriculture which depended on the flood regime of the river. This farming method enabled the BaTonga people to harvest crops twice a year such that they were seldom afflicted by hunger and famine (see for instance, Kwekudee 2014). See the BaTonga settlement pattern in map 4 below:

Map 4: The BaTonga Settlement Pattern

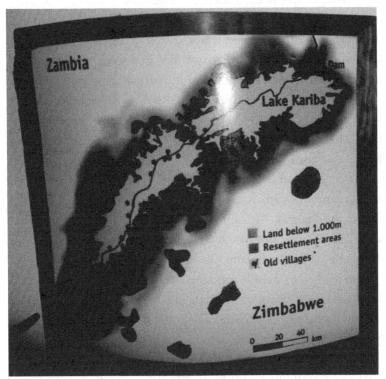

Source: BaTonga Community Museum

As also revealed in the BaTonga settlement pattern map (map. 5) above, the BaTonga people did not only grow their crops in the rich soils along the rivers, but supplemented this in a large part from the rich bounty of these areas through fishing, gathering wild plants, and hunting the many wild animals in the forest.

The BaTonga ethnic group of Zimbabwean side has had their culture got interfered with colonialism very late (see Reynolds and Cousins 1989; Reynolds 1989). For the most part of the 19th century the BaTonga people lived an isolated life and religiously depended on their culture for virtually everything they needed for survival (see for instance, Ncube 2004; Reynolds and Cousins 1989). They supported and sustained their lives through indigenous knowledge and technologies – survival techniques the BaTonga people depended on since time immemorial. They could, for example, fish freely in the Zambezi River; prey at will on animals that came for water drinking along the Zambezi River; and gather fruits and vegetables that were rampant along the River without any restrain from the government. This was possible given that the Zambezi River was rich in almost everything and that all the aforementioned activities were free then. The river, which flows 2 650 km and the fourth largest river in Africa flowing into the Indian Ocean, rises in northwestern Zambia with a catchment area that covers 1 352 000 square kilometres and eight countries namely Angola, Botswana, Malawi, Mozambique, Namibia, Tanzania, Zambia and Zimbabwe before it enters the Indian Ocean in Mozambique at Quelimane.

The BaTonga people remained undisturbed up until the late 1950s when the European settlers in Rhodesia (now Zimbabwe) proposed to build the Kariba Dam with the motive to generate hydro-electric power. The Dam construction was an initiative between the federation of the time between the British who ruled Northern and Southern Rhodesia (now Zambia and Zimbabwe respectively) and Nyasaland (now Malawi) (World Commission on Dams 2000; Columbia Encyclopaedia 2007). The damming of Zambezi River had a number of effects (direct and indirect) not only to the BaTonga people but also to their natural environment they [the BaTonga people] largely depended on. First, large areas of forests were destroyed such that many animals lost their habitats. Second, the local people had to be relocated, displaced from their fishing opportunities and losing the rich alluvial river soil they grew their crops right round the year. In fact, this disrupted the BaTonga people's way of life and had some negative consequences on their livelihoods. Third, the BaTonga people were depersonified with most of their names, religious and cultural values distorted. During an interview with one of the chiefs in Binga, for example, it was revealed to me that the original name of Zambezi River was

42

Kasambezi meaning those who know how to bath in a crocodile infested river. The chief lamented this change by the colonists as he clearly indicated that in their own language, the name "Zambezi" does not mean anything. Forth, through the dominance of the colonial rule in Salisbury, Southern Rhodesia (now Zimbabwe), most of the stranded animals that were rescued – through what they called *Operation Noah* – from the island were relocated to the side of Zimbabwean side while most of the people, to the Zambian side. This greatly affected the family institution of the BaTonga people as in many cases rescued siblings were separated during the Operation, one to become a Zambian national while another becoming Zimbabwean. Recalling what happened during the 1950s when she was separated from her three children who were taken to the Zambian side during the rescue operation, old Yemi lamented:

> I have no good words at all for those colonists! You know how they destroyed our family institutions! I had seven children (raising her fingers up). Three of these were taken to the now Zambian side. Three! Two girls and a boy (she cried). We used even to visit some of our families on the other side of the river freely. That was before the construction of the Dam, and the river was not yet as big as it is today. All this volume was a result of the Dam they constructed. Now when my children want to visit me here they have to go the other way round. And, they need papers (referring to passport).

Fifth, the damming of the Zambezi River meant the blocking of the great Zambezi River, a place where the BaTonga people believed was home to their great river god, the Nyaminyami, who they believed caused anyone who ventured closer the gorge (Kariva) to be sucked into the cavernous depths of the river forever. See figure 3 below showing the image of the Nyaminyami River god I saw in the museum during my fieldwork.

Figure 3: Nyaminyami River god

Source: BaTonga Community Museum

When the BaTonga people heard they were to be displaced, they strongly believed this was going to anger the Nyaminyami so much that he would cause the water in the river to boil and destroy the wall of the dam with floods. Indeed in 1957, only a year into the construction of the dam, the river rose to flood level destroying the white men's equipment and access roads. The following year, 1958, a more severe flood hit the dam wall destroying its main parts, access bridge, the coffer dam, with water passing over the wall at more than 16 million litres a second, a flood which, according to researchers would only happen once in ten thousand years (see for instance, World Commission on Dams 2000). Although the European settlers finally succeeded in building the dam that was officially opened in 1960, everyone including the Europeans who previously did not respect the Nyaminyami River god believed in his power.

When Kariba Dam was finally built, the BaTonga people did not only resisted moving away from the riverside for fearing to displease Nyaminyami, but resisted foreign intangible cultural heritage (e.g. knowledge forms and religion) and material culture (e.g. technologies) in favour of their own. This made the BaTonga culture to remain intact and resilient until at least recently. Unfortunately, this resilience and love of their culture has generally been misconstrued by some quarters to mean underdevelopment, backwardness, naivety, simplicity, among a lot of other negative descriptions and pejorative labellings (see for instance, Munikwa 2011). As Munikwa claim, this refusal of the BaTonga people to adopt foreign cultural values has regrettably been viewed as incapacity to appreciate 'superior' Western culture. It also explains why the BaTonga ethnic group has suffered the nastiest multiple stereotypes at both national and international levels. The stereotypes of the BaTonga people, as those of other African groupings elsewhere, were initially invented by imperial colonisers who upon finding out it difficult to break into their culture ended up developing hatred upon them. The stereotypical thinking of Europe over Africa and the African people in general has always had ulterior motives; it was a ploy bent on demonising, fanning hostility and hatred (Mawere 2014). Interestingly, the BaTonga people have largely remained loyal to their culture as they have always perceived 'development' dictated from outside as repugnant and anti-humane. Sadly, even after national independence in 1980, some ethnic groups in Zimbabwe and many other people elsewhere in the world inherited the stereotyping of the BaTonga thereby propagating and perpetuating the colonial mentality against this group.

As underlined above, the BaTonga people were displaced from the shores of the Zambezi River in the late 1950s when Kariba Dam was built and filled. The forced resettlement resulted in serious disruptions of the socio-economic and cultural environment of the BaTonga people. This, and the many misconceptions about the BaTonga people by outsiders, prompted the post-colonial government of Zimbabwe through its National Museums and Monuments (ZNMM) to assist in promoting their culture through the facilitation of the establishment of the BCM.

Situated in Binga on the shores of Lake Kariba, about 4km from the Zambezi River mainstream, the BCM was established in 2000 and officially opened in 2002 (BCM File no. 4). The construction of the museum was facilitated by a Danish organisation known as the *Mellemfolkeligt Samvirke-Zimbabwe* (MS-Zimbabwe). The museum is rectangular in shape and approximately 15 meters long. It is nicely thatched with grass to depict its rootedness from the local culture, particularly the local BaTonga houses that are grass-thatched. See figure 4 below which shows the BaTonga Community Museum.

Figure 4: The BaTonga Community Museum

The main objective of the museum was to promote and empower the local communities, and most importantly to create awareness about the BaTonga history and culture which is largely embedded in the philosophy of their life; the latter point of which scholars like Rowlands (2008) would consider as restoration of heritage in post-conflict situations. As such, the BCM houses and displays objects drawn from the BaTonga culture. These include the fishing boats, drums, domestic utensils, furnished cultural village, Nyaminyami River god, among others, as supported by the BCM mission statement. See figure 5 below which shows the mission statement of the BaTonga Community Museum.

Figure 5: The Mission Statement of the BCM

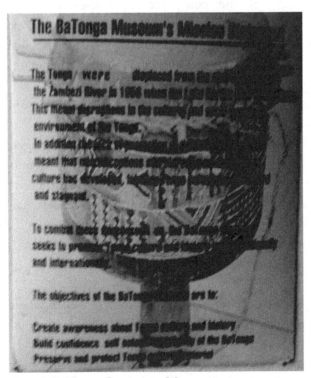

Source: BaTonga Community Museum

As is revealed in the mission statement of the BCM, its main mandate is to showcase the traditions, 'science,' beliefs and ingenuity of the BaTonga people who live in what many people would perceive as a dry, hostile environment. The rich BaTonga history and culture are recorded and captured in the museum.

The Governance and Management of BaTonga Community Museum

Ownership and Management of the Site

The National Museums and Monuments Act Chapter 25:11 (of 1972), provides for the legal protection, maintaining the Archaeological Survey, the national inventory of monuments and sites (UNESCO 2012). In Zimbabwe, the NMMZ, which is under the Ministry of Rural Development, Preservation of National Cultural Heritage (and formerly under the Ministry of Home Affairs), is the entity directly responsible for the management of heritage sites such as the BCM. Funding for the management and conservation of heritage sites comes mainly from the central government with limited income generated by entrance/tour guide fees, accommodation and sale of publications which are used to finance projects at the national level at the discretion of the NMMZ Board of Trustees.

Yet, in the case of the BCM, the ownership and management of the museum is quite complex. If my fieldwork is anything to go by, the majority of the people I interviewed and interacted with, including local leadership, expressed the belief that the BCM belongs to the community. One of the Headmen in Binga, Koba's (not his real name) response is worth noting. He confided to me during an interview on the matter:

The BCM belongs to the community as a whole. It belongs to us! Unfortunately, this is not what is obtaining in reality. It's even confusing not only for me but for many other headmen and community members here in Binga. At one time you hear that the site is a national asset and at another time you hear it belongs to the local community. Truly speaking even the name of the site bears testimony to the fact that the BCM belongs to the local community. But sometimes we are divorced from the site which leaves us with no power and control over the site. Although NMMZ is trying to infuse the local leadership and community members in general in the management and daily activities at the museum, in reality we feel like we are more of stakeholders than owners of the site.

There were a few individuals together with the Curator-in-charge of the museum, Heritage Education Officer, and Tour guide, among others, who argue that the site belongs not only to the community but the government as it is the latter that provided way for its creation and provides instruments for its management. Besides, they argue that it is from the government where funds for managing the site come from. The Curator for the site even gave me a more complex and unique answer to the question on the ownership and management of the BCM. He indicated that the site belongs to the government but the government gives it to the community and the world as a gift and a heritage resource that has to be enjoyed by everyone but most especially the locals.

It appears the confusion on who legitimately owns and has the full mandate to manage the BCM emanates from the nature of Zimbabwe's political system. The Zimbabwean political system is a duality of systems of government namely, customary (also known as traditional leadership) and statutory (also known as modern or bureaucratic government), which are both recognised by the current Constitution of Zimbabwe (of 2013). Meinzen-Dick and Pradhan (2002) argue that the existence of parallel legal systems creates confusion and uncertainty for both local resource users and state appointed functionaries, resulting in "forum shopping"; that is, selective use and application of rules and regulations that suit their particular needs and circumstances.

Yet in Binga Communal Area, as elsewhere in communal areas in Zimbabwe, there is a dual leadership system – traditional leadership and bureaucratic/elected government – that exist side by side. For purposes of this study, traditional leadership shall be used to refer to 'the authorities that existed in pre-colonial through colonial times, which are, at the present time, responsible for governing the welfare of people and the utilisation of natural resources in the countryside' (Mawere 2015: 42). But one might want to understand more on the circumstances surrounding elected government in Zimbabwe in relation to management of natural resources in the rural areas.

Elected government authorities in Zimbabwe were tasked at independence in 1980 to perform the same duties as those of traditional leadership structures. This was part of a process to disempower traditional authority and punish it for its role in collaborating with the colonial government, for example, through tax collection for the later (Makumbe 1998). Scoones and Matose (1993) also argue that Rural District Council Act (RDCA) accords all power to the state and limits that of the local people— traditional leadership—to participate and exercise authority and control in the management of natural resources in their communities. However, it is worth noting that although the chief is now appointed by the President, in contrast to the colonial and pre-colonial periods, a critical look at the chiefs' roles in post-independent Zimbabwe shows that it is indeed a restoration or return to their role during the colonial period, when they were also tasked to supervise headmen, oversee the collection of taxes (on behalf of the colonial government), and ensure proper management of natural resources such as land (cf. Mawere 2015; Makumbe 1998). In terms of the Communal Land Act of 1982, Rural District Councils (RDCs) are the land authorities responsible for the allocation of land within their areas of responsibility. However, this allocation of land by the RDCs is carried out within the confines of traditions and customs which are commonly accepted, and traditional leadership is the custodian of these. In the face of these two systems, heritage resource ownership and management at district level are the responsibility of the district councils through

50

their Rural District Development Committees (RDDCs), comprising elected leaders and technical officers from line ministries. The RDDC is empowered by the RDC through the RDC Act of 1988 (revised 1996) to make by-laws and develop new ones in conjunction with local communities. Yet at the local level, the village assembly or its headmen are in charge of the enforcement of all heritage resource management and conservation by-laws on behalf of the chief. No wonder why the parallel existence of traditional leadership and RDCs has always posed power struggles, and in many cases a crisis in natural resource conservation and management in communal areas of Zimbabwe (see for instance, Makumbe 1998; Hammar 2005; Byers, Cunliffe and Hudak 2001).

During fieldwork, I observed that, in practice, the bureaucratic government structures are not supported by local communities in Binga, yet both systems of leadership are legislatively supported by the following statutes; the revised edition of the Rural District Councils (RDCs) of 1996, the Provincial Councils and Administration Act Number 12, the Traditional Leaders Act (TLA) (Chapter 29, 17), Number 25 of 1998, and the Constitution of Zimbabwe (EISA Report 2007: 79). All these statutes maintain that the head of the state appoints traditional leaders who have been selected at local levels according to customary laws and with the aid of local government, particularly the District Administrator's (DA) office. In Table 2 below, I present the different leadership structures for both the bureaucratic government and traditional structures, who in one way or another are involved in the management of heritage resources.

Table 2. Leadership structures for both the bureaucratic government and traditional structures

Level	Traditional Leadership Authorities	State/Government Leadership Authorities
National Level	President of Council of Chiefs	President and Cabinet
Provincial Level	Council of Chiefs	Provincial Administrator
District Level	Chiefs[2] (in Binga District)	Member of Parliament (MP) District Administrator Rural District Council Chair Rural District Development Committee (for Binga)
Kaani Ward 11	Chief (*Simwami*) Chief's Advisors (*Inkuta/Gobelo*) Headman (*Sibhuku mupati*) Village Head (*Sibhuku*) Homestsead Head (*Mulimunzi/Mwanimunzi*)	Councillor WADCO Ward Committee Village Committee VIDCO Chair VIDCO

From what I gathered during fieldwork, it was apparent that NMMZ and the government are managing the BCM on behalf of the community through provision of funds and expertise on the management in form of workers to look after the site. As the Curator narrated, NMMZ policy, on behalf of the government of Zimbabwe, encourages engagement of local community such that at BCM, there is a Local Community Management Committee. Three of the community members I had the

---

[2] There are seventeen Chiefs in Binga District. These are Binga, Sikalenge, Saba, Siansali, Dobola, Sinasengwe, Sinampande, Siabuwa, Sinamunsanga, Pashu, Sinakatenge, Kavula, Sinamagonde, Siamupa, Siachilaba, Sinamwenda, and Sinakoma. BaTonga Community Museum is under the jurisdiction of Chief Binga.

privilege to interact with, however, expressed that they are sometimes only called to meetings at the BCM for information. While the headmen and community members generally agreed that they are regularly informed on certain issues and activities pertaining to the site, some employees at the BCM indicated that locals are mostly involved in the relationship between the local community and the site especially on issues pertaining to culture. Nevertheless, on other issues, only technocrats working at the museum are directly involved. On this note, it becomes difficult to ascertain that the local community is totally involved when they are only involved in cultural issues and excluded in socio-economic development issues of their society. This reality even makes one to ascertain that the ownership and management of the BCM is complex. Besides, it reveals that the site belongs to the local community yet managed by NMMZ on behalf of the government. In fact, though the local community is sometimes involved in the daily management of the heritage site, it remains clear that it has no legal basis to lay total claim over the site. This, in a way, compromises sustainability and development of local communities around the BCM as it implies that the cultural heritage site has become a state property managed by outsiders instead of insiders who are directly affected by the site. Such a scenario also compromises participation and downplays potential and contribution of the local community members to the cultural heritage site.

Conclusion

This chapter has provided context for my specific study by examining the experiences of the BaTonga people of Binga Communal Area both before and after the construction of Kariba Dam along the Zambezi River. This historical background together with an account on how I entered into the field site was meant to shed more light on the continuing agency and relevance of BaTonga culture even after the post-Kariba Dam era. It is on the basis of this background that the chapter has argued that the culture of the BaTonga people is embedded in their philosophy of life as they experience the world on daily basis.

While locating the study of effects of cultural heritage sites in contemporary Zimbabwe, the chapter has also looked at the ownership and management challenges and complexities surrounding the BCM. It concludes that the existence of duality of leadership structures – bureaucratic government and traditional leadership – that are both involved in the management of heritage resources compromises community participation and socio-economic potentials of cultural heritage sites in Zimbabwe.

The next chapter provides a general overview of the research findings by addressing questions of agency, effects and effectiveness as articulated by community members (or research participants) and giving a sense of the commonalities and differences between responses by the research participants.

Chapter 4

The BaTonga Community Museum, community and agency

Introduction

The discussion in the preceding chapter has revealed that the community around the BCM though acknowledged being involved in many of the activities of the heritage site, have no legal basis to lay claim over the ownership of their heritage site. However, according to the Curator-in-charge of the site, NMMZ Act 25:11 stipulates that NMMZ cannot work successfully without the involvement of traditional leadership. This is because, traditional leadership is directly involved in the conservation and protection of heritage resources as well as the education of the public given their role as sole custodians of cultural heritage sites.

To ensure that the agency of the BCM and that of the BaTonga as a people is recognised and articulated, the NMMZ through the BCM set up a local committee called BaTonga Museum Local Committee (BMLC) which comprises local people who are usually the chiefs' representatives. The BMLC, which is understood as the voice of the people, report back to their respective chiefs and the community at large, all developments, gatherings, and activities going on at the BCM. The BMCL is normally called for consultation by the BCM at least once every month but depending on the events available and availability of resources. This is an expression towards the acknowledgement that the museum belongs to the local people. Besides, it is a gesture towards empowerment and to guarantee sustainability in local communities. This relates to what the Curator of the BCM emphasised during an interview:

One of our mandates, and indeed the biggest one, is to empower the communities around this area; to ensure that their voices are heard; to ensure that their culture is well appreciated and respected; to ensure that talent based on cultural backgrounds is promoted. We believe this is the best way to guarantee sustainability and cultural valorisation. More importantly, this mandate is in line with the Zimbabwe National Culture Policy (ZNCP).

As alluded to by the Curator, the Zimbabwe National Culture Policy emphasises the need to understand and respect who Africans are as a people, foster social cohesion, unity and sustainability thus: 'in respecting and always remembering who we are as an African people, with unique African identities, and fostering respect for the same, remains one of the surest ways of improving people's livelihoods, and ensuring social cohesion, unity and peace as people mutually striving to empower themselves using their heritage to create sustainable livelihoods —now and in the future—in a mutually supportive environment' (Zimbabwe National Culture Policy 2015: 15). The Zimbabwe National Culture Policy is not only emphasising community involvement in cultural issues but is reminding us of the connection between memory and material culture. As Rowlands argues,

> memory traces exist as marks which are not conscious, but by appropriate stimuli they might be energised long afterwards. As a longing to regain a lost trace, repetition in form has no meaning except as a compulsion to engage change in a return to a sense of origin. Object traditions, rather than language or speech, serve as the only means of gaining access to such unconscious traces, and they do so by allowing direct re-engagement with past experience in ways that are prevented in language. The reason therefore why heirlooms, souvenirs and photo-graphs have this particular capacity to evoke and to establish continuities with past experience is precisely because, as a material symbol rather

than verbalised meaning, they provide a special form of access to both individual and group unconscious processes (Rowlands 1993: 144).

Understood in Rowlands' terms, memory is a longing to re-engage with the past which might have been experienced directly or indirectly. This understanding necessitates participation by all communities linked to a cultural heritage site such as the BCM, so that they are afforded the opportunity to 'evoke, establish continuities' with the past, and engage with their past-present through material culture – objects – that link them with the past, present, and future. This is important given that there is a strong relationship between memory and cultural transmission (Kuechler 1987). The participation and connection between the material objects in the BCM and the community members/people involved is possible through agency exercised during interaction between the two parties. Besides, it is possible on the basis that 'objects of a durable kind assert their own memories, their own forms of commentary and therefore come to possess their own personal trajectories' (Ibid) or what Kopytoff (1986) termed personal biography of things. This is because besides the material objects in the museum such as the BaTonga hunting weapons, fishing materials, domestic utensils, among others, the Binga Communal Area is 'peopled' in many other things –wild animals and thick well conserved vegetation – things I believe have a social life of their own and affect both local and visitors in different ways. Some of the wild animals such as ducker, hare, guinea fowl, and jaguar are, for example, hunted by people for meat while it is from the locally conserved environment that the local people get raw materials to make their artefacts. Given that the people around the BCM are actively involved in the conservation of the environment – habitat of the animals and source of raw materials – while people depend on the animals for meat, I argue that there is interdependence between humans, the environment, and the animals in Binga Communal Area.

Nevertheless, some community members still felt that local communities around the BCM are not fully engaged in the co-management of the site, worse still to take ownership of the museum for their development projects for their mutual and inclusive benefit. One of the traditional leaders I interviewed, for instance, expressed his discontentment on the involvement of traditional leadership in the co-management of the museum in a manner that uphold and preserve everyone's human dignity and sustainable livelihoods. One of the chiefs in Binga, Chief Ndeka (not his real name), for instance, registered his displeasure thus:

Traditional leaders such as us, chiefs, are not really involved in the strict sense of the term 'traditional leadership involvement' but only consulted on issues and events to do with traditional culture and management of heritage resources outside the BCM as if we are only stakeholders. We are not stakeholders; we are the owners of the BCM. But, we are actively involved, for example, to protect our respective areas from veld fires. This makes us believe that the government through NMMZ and in particular the BCM only need us as free sources of labour.

What chief Ndeka notes here is critical. He reveals that while traditional leaders are for co-management and total ownership of the BCM, NMMZ and the current management of the site feel that there are certain areas of management that only require professionally trained experts to handle. The view by chief Ndeka shows that conflict seems a major issue in community development and sustainability of government driven projects in Zimbabwe as in most parts of Africa. This is the same observation that Mowforth and Munt (2003) note when they postulate that: 'There is a vast body of work that demonstrates that local communities in 3rd World countries reap few benefits from cultural tourism because they have little control over the ways in which the industry is developed, they cannot match the financial resources available to external investors, and their views are rarely heard' (p. 211). This is in spite of the warning by some scholars and researchers that denying locals a voice and opportunity to reap benefits from their heritage has the same effect as chopping, cutting, dissolving, crushing, and burning which are all acts of forgetting and not remembering (see for instance, Rowlands 1993).

Mowforth and Munt are in fact of the view that despite the inherent link existent between cultural heritage conservation and sustainable development, the great potential of many cultural heritage sites across the world is still not sufficiently harnessed for contributing to socio-economic development most especially in the so-called developing countries. Similarly, Chauke (2003) argues that the insufficient harnessing of potentials of cultural heritage sites is largely a result of some professionals who mystify their work as a scientific endeavour that the local communities cannot and have no capacity to contribute to. Thus, it is because of this attitude by some professionals that many communities feel sidelined and excluded to the extent that expected benefits from cultural heritage sites are rarely enjoyed. Yet, we might remind ourselves of what Rowlands (2008: 150, emphasis original) warns us: 'Inequalities and disproportionate access to such resources *as the museum or cultural centres* are accompanied by obvious dangers of regionalism and stranger/autochthony conflicts.'

While some traditional leaders felt they were not actively involved in the running of the BCM, other local community members were of a different view. They believed that as a community they were involved and actively participated in a manner that stimulated sustainable development and take into account agency of things and in particular how "things" mediate social agency between and amongst themselves. This [active] participation – participatory approach – by community members in BaTonga community indeed brings out the peculiar nature and resolution of contentions or conflict that normally arise in sustainability of many government driven community development projects in Zimbabwe and beyond. Jeryson, a man in his mid-twenties from a nearby Siabuwa Community, for example, had this to say during a group focus discussion:

> The local community around here is actively involved in activities at the BCM, which helps us greatly to conserve our culture and appreciate who we are as a people. There are, for example, cultural dancing groups, craftsmen groups, skin curing drum and making groups, among others. We all exhibit our artefacts at the museum for free and in many cases, the museum buys our artefacts for display in the museum. I am, for instance, a craftsman and have a number of objects on display in the museum. And, my friend here, Jose is a drum maker who likewise has a number of drums on display in the Crafts and Arts Centre there. So, for me everyone participates not only in the management but many other activities at the museum as long as s/he wants to be involved.

The vignette by Jeryson above resonates with the vision and mission statement for the BCM in fig. 7 as contributing to the awareness of the BaTonga culture, education, economic viability and development, in particular tourism. In Binga, there are various cultural performance groups working in theatre, music and dance, particularly in or around the BCM. This makes the BCM a focal point for both tangible and intangible heritage such that the community and the government of Zimbabwe look to it for encouraging the development of African crafts, dance, and music performance besides economic development. And, for scholars like Rowlands (2008: 149, emphasis original), 'if museums and cultural heritage have a role in developing a more self-conscious strategy for *promoting awareness of the society's culture and socio-economic development*, it presumably should be to respond to demands to attach value to skills and resources, presumably for those who were suppressed or ignored in the past settler/ indigenous hierarchy [...] with limited access of the minority to "civilisation" through education.'

Also, what Jeryson reported supports my argument in chapter two that tracing the effects of heritage sites enables us to recognise what Heath calls 'non-human agency'. It also reconciles the effects with different conceptions of nature, personhood and relationships amongst people and with cultural objects. In the section below, I examine the nexus between community participation, promotion of culture, and sustainable development.

The nexus between culture, community participation and sustainable development

In heritage discourse, community participation is arguably the key factor to promote culture, ensure sustainable development and community empowerment in any human community. As Amartya Sen (1990) summarises, community empowerment is the ability of people to lead a long life, to enjoy good health, to have access to the world's stock of knowledge and information, to participate in cultural life of their community, to have sufficient income to buy food, cloth, shelter and to participate in decisions that directly affect their lives and their community. Talking in relation to heritage, Marshall (2002) understands community participation as the inclusion of indigenous people and other communities in various areas of archaeology and heritage practice and interpretation as site management and conservation. In the case of this thesis, community participation is the engagement of communities in activities taking place at cultural heritage sites such as the BCM. Pearce and Atikins (1993) would agree with both Sen and Marshall as they add that active participation of the community in cultural life and decisions that affect their lives leads to community empowerment. In much the same way, Eboireme (2009) suggests that one sure way of achieving sustainability is linking the management of cultural heritage to the social and economic needs of people living in communities adjacent to archaeological sites in historic settlements. I add that participation in previously marginalised communities like Binga is more urgent now than ever as it is the only surest way to guarantee empowerment, to promote appreciation of their culture, and to ensure that their agency is recognised. The consensus of the members of the BaTonga community is that recognising agency of both the BaTonga as a people and that of BCM has the potency to promote sustainable development as full potential of both the people and other cultural resources are realised. These views are aptly represented by the opinion of an elderly woman, Mbuya Tabona of a local community, Manjolo who in an interview on the matter had this to say:

> It is important that we take part in the activities of the BCM, our museum, and indeed we do especially when it comes to cultural activities there. This is important to us. You know the objects housed by that museum have life and communicate with us, the BaTonga people, in a way that enriches us; in a way that makes us proud as a people; in a way that makes us understand ourselves fully as a people; in a way that connects us with our past; and in a way that ensures that the future of our children is in the direction we want it to be. So there is more to life in that museum in as much as there is life in me and you (looking at me).

As Mbuya Tabona shared her opinion with me, her village mates, Mbuya Tabitha and Modina could be seen nodding their heads in approval. They plainly agreed with Mbuya Tabona's view on how as villagers and owners of the BCM, they should continue interacting with their museum.

Surely as told by Tabona, during fieldwork I observed that the BCM was indeed involved in a number of cultural activities. I happened to witness, for example, a basketry workshop that was carried out at the museum. See figure 6 below which shows baskets being made during a workshop at the BaTonga Community Museum.

Figure 6: Crafts being made during workshop at the BCM

Other cultural activities that were reported to be often carried out at the museum included drumming and dancing.

Besides, what Tabona tells us in the vignette above resonates with Warnier's study of heritage issues, including the human body, largely in terms of material culture (see for instance, Warnier 2001; 2005; 2007; Salpeteur and Warnier 2013). Warnier considers material objects, for example the human body, as containers with inside and outside, openings and surfaces. Besides, he argues that such material objects being containers are actors in the material world that are constantly in a state of becoming given that by acting in a material world the object – or what he calls body 'supplements itself with innumerable surfaces and containers by means of which it extends beyond its own physical limits' (Warnier 2005: 186). Thus, in as much as Warnier talks of objects such as human bodies as containers with inside and outside surfaces, Tabona considers the BCM as a container with objects capable of assuming agency. This means

Tabona, as with Tabitha and Modina, would agree with Warnier that material culture is an essential component of the body or 'sensori-motoricity' as Warnier himself likes to call it. On this note, I argue with both (Tabona and Warnier) that material culture such as a museum – the BCM, for example – has an envelope and contents that like the museum itself are also containers. This is possibly one other reason why Tabona recognises objects in the museum as material culture that should be analysed and understood wholesomely if one is to recognise their agency fully. In this regard, Tabona agrees with Warnier that material culture in which containers, inside, outside, openings and surfaces could be found are all relevant in understanding the body and its conducts with other 'acting subjects.'

Interestingly, Tabona's words also reverberates Kopytoff's (1982; 1986) cultural biographical approach – an approach of studying cultures that allows the analysis of relationships between persons and things as a process of social transformation that involves a series of changes in status. Like Kopytoff's (1986) argument that things are culturally constructed and reconstructed in much the same way people are culturally (re-)constructed, Tabona teaches us that in the BaTonga society, things take part in a culture, constructed and reconstructed through time. Besides, Tabona's vignette teaches us one other important thing that escapes Kopytoff's approach; that things have life and by tracing a biography of a thing we recognise its agency as well. In fact, the emergent field of material culture studies has underscored the extent to which objects just like persons lead social lives, hence I agree with Tabona that things have agency which enable them to transgress the usual boundaries between them and persons. This understanding enhances Kopytoff's approach to what I call 'critical kopytoffian approach – an approach I described in the preceding paragraph.

Moreover, Tabona also underlines the need for community involvement. Fortunately, it is now generally agreed among scholars that community participation in the management of cultural heritage sites is an ideal scenario if sustainable development is to be ever achieved (see for instance, MacManamon 2000; Marshall 2002; Pwiti and Chirikure 2008; Kuper 2003; Damm 2005, Rossler and Saouma-Forero (1999), and Watkins (2003). Marshall (2002), for example, argues that community involvement has become a global trend and it has impacted positively on the lives of many indigenous and local communities in Southern Africa. The point to note is that where cultural heritage sites which have benefits yet will have been kept out of the public would be addressed by local participation thereby promoting sustainable development. This also explains why the World Heritage Committee (WHC) now advocates for community participation in the management of cultural heritage for sustainable development (Rossler and Saouma-Forero 1999). Rossler and Saouma-Forero (1999) even remind us that before putting any cultural landscape properties on the prestigious World Heritage List, the WHC stipulates that there should be evidence of community participation. This underscores the importance of community involvement and recognition of the agency of both community members and heritage resources.

Conclusion

This chapter, which is a general overview of my research findings, has examined the interplay between agency and the BaTonga community. While emphasising the need for community involvement in museum management and activities, the chapter has addressed questions of effects and effectiveness as articulated by community members (or research participants) thereby giving a sense of the commonalities and differences between responses by the research participants. Besides, the chapter has demonstrated that there is nexus between culture and the owners of a culture and agency. The next chapter, which is a follow-up of the present chapter, focuses on the socio-economic effects of the BCM.

Chapter 5

Socio-economic Effects of the BaTonga Community Museum

Introduction

The effects and even effectiveness of the BCM are felt differently by different community members though all the participants I had privilege to interact with confirmed that the museum had socio-economic effects to the Binga Community. It is worth emphasising that effects are either positive or negative. Besides, as explained in chapter 1, effects are in most cases difficult to measure using conventional methods given that they are wider than effectiveness to include both intended and unintended outcomes. On this note, we are reminded of what Mcquail (1979: 8) teaches us when he says 'we can distinguish between effects and effectiveness, the former referring to consequences [...] whether intended or not, the latter to the capacity to achieve given objectives, whether this be attracting large audiences or influencing opinions and behaviour.' In the next section, I discuss further the findings of my study but focusing on specific socio-economic contributions of the BCM to local communities around the site.

The BaTonga Community Museum as a socio-economic development factor

As argued by scholars, there is interconnection between cultural heritage and sustainable development in so far as cultural heritage can be used by the community as an economic resource and drive towards sustainable development (see for instance, Marshall 2002; Pwiti and Chirikure 2008; Kuper 2003; Damm 2005; Rossler and Saouma-Forero1999, and Watkins

2003). From what I harvested during fieldwork, it was clear that cultural heritage can be used by local communities as an economic resource to generate revenue and create employment in several other sectors of the economy. In the sections below, I discuss the specific contributions to socio-economic development of the communities around the BCM.

Heritage Tourism

One of the most visible aspects of the contribution of culture to local development in Binga District is tourism. Mr Mudenda, one of the workers at the BCM, concurs when he notes:

Our museum here attracts a significant number of tourists from within Zimbabwe and from abroad. The objects that the museum houses, as you can see, are culturally rich besides their aesthetic value that they attract people from all walks of life. Although our museum is located in one of the areas considered as the most remote in the country, we still manage to attract tourists that come to northern Zimbabwe to visit other beautiful areas such as Victoria Falls and Hwange National Park. These people buy artefacts from people around here when they visit the place besides appreciating our culture.

As could be seen, Mr Mudenda is talking of heritage tourism, which represents a major potential for local and national economic development, to areas such as Binga. What Mr Mudenda alluded to was also supported by what I observed in the visitor's record and inventory book for the period between January and July 2015, particularly on how much the museum harvested from tour guide fees, donations and government grants. The tour guide fees for national and international visitors are US$2/person and US$5/person respectively. From what I got during fieldwork, the BCM gets most of its local visitors from education institutions (schools, colleges and universities) and international visitors from countries around the world but mainly from Europe. In Tables 3 and 4 below, I provide data for the number of visitors (both local and international) and proceeds from the BCM for the months January to July 2015:

Table 3: Demographic data for visitors at the BaTonga Community Museum

Month	Local (from within Zimbabwe)	International
January	10	17
February	11	15
March	20	9
April	15	18
May	35	2
June	30	0
July	20	6
Total	**141**	**67**

Source: BaTonga Community Museum File

Besides, the existence of a number of lodges and restaurants around the site – along the Zambezi River – was further referred to by Mr Mudenda as a clear testimony of how tourists are spending their monies on local business. During fieldwork, I happened to meet one of the visitors of the BCM, Mr Geertz from the Netherlands. He was with his family –his wife Mirjan and two daughters Jane and Jessy – on holiday. When I talked to him about what he thought of the BCM, Mr Geertz could not hide his joy for having had the opportunity to visit the museum. He thus noted:

Table 4: Monthly proceeds harvested by the BaTonga Community Museum between January and July 2015

Month	Tour guide fees (US$)	Donations (US$)	Government Grants (US$)	Monthly Total (US$)
January	$105	$200	-	$305
February	$97	$ 250	-	$347
March	$85	$150	-	$235
April	$120	$100	-	$220
May	$80	$20	$800	$900
June	$60	$20	-	$80
July	$70	$200	-	$270

Source: BaTonga Community Museum File

I travel a lot but from what I saw in this museum (pointing to the museum as we were standing outside the museum), I can safely say that the BaTonga culture is one of the richest cultures in this country and indeed Africa and the world. I have seen a lot of well-crafted artefacts neatly displayed in the museum. The artefacts exhibit the richness, resilience and deftness of the BaTonga culture. I really appreciate the creativity in this culture. The chairs they make, for example, clearly exhibit a high degree of creativity; creativity of a people who closely interact with the environment around them. It is a wonderful culture, and I am really enjoying being here with my family.

As Mr Geertz was speaking, I could see his wife Mirjan nodding her head in approval. His two daughters were also smiling as their father was commenting on what they saw in the BCM. Mr Geertz went on to donate US$200 to the museum encouraging the Curator and his team to keep on promoting their cultural heritage. The gesture by Mr Geertz together with the information on how much the BCM harvested from visitors and donations echo with observations by scholars such as Marshall (2002), Timothy and Nyaupane (2009), Rowley (2002), and Rypkema's (2009) who all argue that cultural heritage sites generate revenue through tourism. Timothy and Nyaupane (2009), writing on cultural heritage and tourism in developing world, for example, pointed out that visits to cultural and historical resources have become one of the largest and fastest growing sectors of tourism industry. Rypkema (2009), who researched on cultural tourism in Europe also observed that heritage tourism is an important component of local economic activity in many places in Europe. Besides, he observed that cultural tourism is a major contribution to tourism in general and is currently among the fastest growing segment of the tourism sector. Elsewhere in Zimbabwe, Ndoro (2001) and Fontein (2006) observe that Great Zimbabwe world heritage site represents a success story of local economic empowerment through promotion of cultural tourism; hence the contribution of heritage sites to local development. In their research on Chibvumani Ruins in southeastern Zimbabwe, Sagiya, Mawere and Mubaya (2013) argue that heritage sites also contribute immensely to the enrichment of both the spiritual and material culture helps to boost the country's economy and alleviate poverty among local communities around the site.

Yet, some local visitors and locals I interacted with had some mixed feelings about the contribution of heritage tourism. A local visitor, Tengo's (not her real name) words during my interview with her on the matter are worth noting:

There is no doubt that the BCM is contributing a lot in terms of cultural tourism, local livelihoods and employment. However, my observations during the past three days I have been here are that there are a lot immoral activities such as prostitution going on as a result of the presence of the BCM. I saw last night, for example, a young local girl making love along the shores. It seems it's the culture of all places frequented by distant people especially international visitors. I have witnessed the same at Victoria Falls.

As could be seem from Tengo's observations, not all effects of the BCM are positive. These developments were confirmed by many other people I interacted with during fieldwork. Hence, while the mission for the BCM is to promote and showcase the BaTonga culture, some unintended effects such as cultural decadence also end up obtaining thereby giving credence to Kopytoff's argument that relationships between persons and things is a process of social transformation that involves a series of changes in status.

Employment

The existence of a cultural heritage site in a community normally creates employment opportunities directly or otherwise. See Table 5 below showing the local employment statistics:
As Rafamatanantsoa (2012) observes, benefits (direct or indirect) of cultural heritage sites to community are both economic and social and these are job creation with subsequent unemployment rate reduction, income generation and poverty alleviation, reduction in the emigration rate, non-erosive development, preservation of cultural heritage by means of self-sustained development due to material component-based strategies. People, including locals, are directly employed to help manage and conduct daily activities at the site which in turn help them to sustain themselves and their families. At the BCM, for

example, I observed that there are seven people in direct employment, of which, six of these are locals. Only one, who is the Curator, is not local. Of the local employees, I however observed that there was gender imbalance in the employment thereby failing to give equal opportunities to both sexes. Alice, one of the female employees at the museum, for example, expressed her worry on this imbalance when she said:

Table 5: Local employment statistics

Area	Local Employment	Outside Employment	Percentage of Local Employment
NMMZ	6	1	67%
Restaurant/Shop Outlets	24	5	82.8%
Dance, Arts & Crafts	43	-	100%
Craft Centre	2	-	100%

This museum is helping the community in many ways including creation of employment. I am, however, worried by the imbalance between male and female members in some of the sectors directly linked to our museum. At this museum, for example, we are seven in total yet only two of us are women. And, I feel this is under-representing women in this area.

I agree with Alice that this kind of scenario is likely to impact negatively on the rural community development of Binga Communal Area as it does not create scope for full and equitable participation and enjoyment by all citizens in the country's heritage and cultural expressions.

I further observed that many other local community members are employed indirectly – in induced jobs as is reflected in table 4 above. Induced jobs are those that are performed by persons using cultural heritage as a source for example arts and crafts, cultural industries and even some types of non-cultural activities (Greffe 2004). In the case of the BCM, induced jobs include those by members of the community involved in skin curing, drum making, drumming and dancing, batik/bleaching, culture talks, children art, basketry, and wood curving. A different scenario from the one I described above was observed in indirect employment. I observed that there are more women in indirect employment than men. The underlying point however, remains that cultural heritage sites create employment opportunities to local communities.

It is worth underlining that induced jobs are not only unique to the BCM. A study by Ndoro (2001; 2005) on Great Zimbabwe National Monument reveals that the monument provides the only viable development and employment opportunities. Ndoro goes on to argue that in 1991-2 drought period in Zimbabwe, more than 70% of the families within ten kilometre radius of Great Zimbabwe cultural heritage site directly or indirectly derived their income from the sale of curios to the tourists. Elsewhere, it is well documented that almost 3.5 million jobs in Europe are directly and indirectly sustained by the cultural heritage sector and more than 20% of the 1995 European labour force was employed in fields related to the sector (see for instance, Greffe 2005). All these have positive effects towards sustainability. I argue, therefore, that through provision of employment opportunities especially to the local members of the community, sustainability is also ensured.

Small business

Besides cultural heritage tourism and employment opportunities, small business is another socio-economic benefit that local communities derive from cultural heritage sites. In many tourist resort areas in Zimbabwe such as heritage sites, small businesses are fast becoming one of the main sources of livelihood for locals. Examining economic patterns of resort towns, Katherine Crewe (2011) observes that tourism is the main export in a resort town economy, with most residents of the area working in the tourism or resort industry. It should, however, be underlined that while socio-economic benefits are easy to realise in some businesses, they are not in others. In the case of cultural tourism, for example, socio-economic benefits are easy to realise nowadays due to the fact that the concept of cultural heritage goes beyond the site itself to include relationship between heritage and small businesses around the site. In the case of communities around the BCM, many of them benefit (directly or otherwise) from revenue generated from the village sale as well as sale of many of their Crafts and Arts Centre at the BCM. The small businesses around the museum include coffee shops, retail shops, crafts shops, restaurants, skin turners, drum makers, and clothing, among others. Some illicit business practices such as commercial sex (what is generally known as prostitution) and drug peddling were also reported to be slowly taking place especially between locals and visitors (or tourists) in the area. I should be quick, however, to note that I did not personally witness the reported illicit businesses perhaps due to the limited time I spend in the field and low levels at which the businesses are still taking place.

From my interaction with some of the people involved in the legitimate businesses mentioned above, it was revealed that the businesses benefit a lot from sales they get from visitors at the BCM. This is because when people come to visit the museum, they normally move around buying items from the local businesses. Fig. 7 shows some of the villagers' crafts on display and sale at the Crafts and Art Centre just a few metres from the museum.

Figure 7: Crafts on display in the Crafts and Art Centre

Educational training

Cultural heritage sites benefit societies – both individuals and institutions – in various ways of which educational benefit is one. Greffe (2004) explained how different people benefit from world heritage sites. He argues that to individuals, cultural heritage sites satisfy a variety of needs as artistic, aesthetic, cognitive and even recreation, for owner of public and private monuments, it is a means of mobilising resources necessary for the conservation of monuments. I add that cultural heritage sites also benefit institutions such as institutions through provision of placements for work-related learning. At the BCM, for example, at least two students from various universities around the country are attached for work-related learning. In this regard, the site is not only acting as a cultural but an educational resource. Educating and raising people's awareness of the physical and socio-cultural environment are fundamental to achieving sustainable development (Chirikure *et al* 2010). During the time I carried out my fieldwork, there were two students attached for work related learning at the BCM, both from Midlands State University in Zimbabwe. One of the students, Geoffrey (not his real name) confided in me:

> During an interview with the two students, it was revealed that they had come to the site to learn more about its culture, both material and intangible culture of the BaTonga people. I have been here for five months now since March. I enjoy being here as I am learning lots of new things [...] And, I believe my understanding of tangible and intangible culture is being enriched day-by-day as my work-related learning progresses.

The Curator-in-charge of the BCM also informed me that one of his roles at the museum was to carry out outreaches to schools, where they normally run quiz competitions on cultural aspects of the BaTonga people. However, he added that due to financial constrains they had only managed to run one quiz competition against their target of two competitions per term. Elsewhere, a study by Pwiti and Chirikure (2008) shows that at Great Zimbabwe National Monument, school children were often brought to the site to learn more about its archaeology and culture.

Environmental benefits

Besides the many benefits discussed above, the BCM is benefiting the area through its staunch promotion of environmental conservation. In fact BaTonga Heritage Site can be argued to be successful when it comes to managing the environment in the area. During fieldwork, I witnessed thick forests around the BCM. When I asked how this was made possible, it was revealed to me that conservation of the forests around the museum and indeed in Binga Communal Area in general was largely successful due to active involvement of traditional leadership and local community members in conservation activities. The forests around the museum were, for example, a successfully conserved chiefly because of the museum's inclusion and close working with local communities and traditional leaders as custodians of not only culture but the environment around them. As the Curator pointed out during one of the interviews I carried out with him:

> Traditional leadership is at the forefront of ensuring sustainable conservation of the environment and as such we support this taking stock of the environment as one of the surest ways of ensuring that development now and in the future. In fact, it is one of NMMZ's policy guides that we together with the local community conserve the site for both prosperity and sustainability now and in the future, hence our inclination towards working with traditional leadership in most if not all our projects including promotion of sustainable conservation in this area.

The idea being put forward by the Curator is that traditional cultural values promote the balance between the natural and human worlds. This balance, if achieved, can contribute towards achieving development objectives. It is the same vision that the World Commission on Environment and Development (1987) has, as revealed in its report, that local and indigenous knowledge systems and environmental management practices provide valuable insight and tools for tackling ecological challenges, preventing the loss of biodiversity, reducing land degradation and mitigating the effects of climate change.

Conclusion

The present chapter has addressed more particular themes about effects and/or socio-economic contribution of the BCM to local communities around the museum. Yet, given that some benefits are direct and others are indirect as have been seen in the preceding discussion, it is apparent that distinguishing effects and effectiveness is complex. This is normally compounded by the fact that cultural heritage sites are always in the process of becoming as community members around the sites and visitors alike try to make sense of the world around them. In the next and last chapter I provide a synthetic and overview of (and conclusion to) the thesis by integrating the theory and evidence of the socio-economic effects of the cultural heritage site, the BCM, as discussed in previous chapters. The chapter also underlines the contribution of the thesis to existing knowledge in cultural heritage studies in the light of critical Kopytoffian perspective adopted and the ways in which this perspective can be enhanced.

Chapter 6

The BCM on the Move:
Some Socio-economic lessons

This book critically explored the socio-economic contribution and effects of cultural heritage sites on the livelihoods of local inhabitants of Binga Community –known as the BaTonga people – who live around the cultural heritage site of BCM. To unravel the nuances and subtleties around Zimbabwe's cultural heritage sites, the study has examined the effects and socio-economic contribution of the BCM to the people living in the vicinity of the site. It was underlined that unpacking the effects of cultural heritage sites such as the BCM is useful in rethinking social networks and strategies for sustainable development in the country and more specifically in view of the BaTonga people of Binga. In this whole attempt, the study quested to expose to the twilight zone the different angles from which cultural heritage sites could affect [positively or otherwise] locals in Zimbabwe; to examine how locally generated knowledge could be legitimised and harnessed for both the human and environmental good; to foster 'ethno-science' (Altieri 1995); and to deploy in practice 'symmetrical anthropology' (Latour 1993, 2007) – a novel anthropology that practically moves beyond the nature/culture divide and is open-ended, thereby closing the theoretical and practical research gaps around cultural heritage sites in Zimbabwe.

In light of the above highlighted objectives and those enunciated in chapter 1 of this book, the study has adopted as its theoretical framework a cultural biographical approach (Kopytoff 1982, 1986; Kopytoff and Miers 1977) – an approach of studying cultures that allows the analysis of relationships between persons and things as a process of social transformation that involves a series of changes in status. Yet, in so doing, the study has underlined, using data harvested from the BCM, the fact that no theoretical perspective can capture social realities in all situations. In particular, this book has shown that while it adopts the Kopytoffian model/theory, it differs from the normal Kopytoffian theory on the basis that Kopytoff does not explicitly argue that things have life as has been done in the present thesis. To demonstrate the extent to which I differ with Kopytoff's cultural biographical approach, this thesis has articulately and explicitly argued, using fieldwork data, that by tracing a biography of a thing we recognise its agency as well. It has been through the careful analysis of agency of these things that I examine the effects and socio-economic contribution of the BCM to communities surrounding the site. The present chapter, thus, provides a synthetic overview of the book and, in particular, seeks to draw the connections between the theoretical framing of the thesis (namely, a critical Kopytoffian perspective) and the fieldwork-based evidence pertaining to socio-economic effects of cultural heritage sites, particularly the BCM, on human lives.

I should be quick, however, to note that the chapter, as the book as a whole, does not seek to prove or disprove the ongoing relevance of Kopytoffian perspective on the study of cultural heritage sites in contemporary world (and specifically Zimbabwe) as, in a sympathetically critical way, I have already argued for the relevance of the perspective in understanding biography of things in and surrounding heritage sites. Rather, in a more explicit manner and using fieldwork-based evidence, I have, in this book, tried to show the different ways in which study of effects and socio-economic contributions using Kopytoffian perspective illuminates the multi-dimensional aspect of cultural heritage sites. It should be underscored that this framework was deployed simply as a theoretical guide for understanding effects and socio-economic contributions of heritage. It is hoped that, by doing so, the book contributes to deepening our understanding of the complexities around cultural heritage sites governance, effects, effectiveness and socio-economic contributions to local livelihoods and sustainable development.

As alluded to in chapter 1, the present thesis began as a quest to examine and understand empirically the effects of cultural heritage sites, governance and socio-economic contributions of the sites, by adopting a Kopytoffian perspective. Though I highlighted the inadequacy of Kopytoff's cultural biographical approach particularly its failure to explicitly recognise that things have life and by tracing a biography of a thing we recognise their agency as well, there was strong reason to believe right from the start that Kopytoff's thinking would be of significant value to my study given that the analysis of agency in cultural heritage sites contexts such as those of the BCM allows us to understand the effects and socio-economic contribution of heritage sites. The findings from my fieldwork presented in chapters 3, 4, and 5, I would argue, provided further justification for this claim. In fact the fieldwork for this book has demonstrated that the emergent field of material culture studies underscores the extent to which cultural material objects – things – just like persons lead social lives which make them exercise agency that enable them to transgress the usual boundaries between them and persons thereby allowing their effects to be recognised. I have already argued that this understanding of cultural material objects as described here enhances Kopytoff's approach to what I have referred to as 'critical Kopytoffian approach' – an approach I discussed in chapters 1, 2, and 4 of this book.

In addition to the above, the present thesis has emphasised the role of cultural heritage sites in fostering sustainable development. It has been underscored that generally speaking, sustainability of cultural heritage is much more difficult to determine as compared to that of natural heritage (see Kiriama *et al.* 2010; Moscardo 2001; Faulkner *et al.* 2001). To substantiate this claim, I have made reference to Kiriama *et al* (2010) who, for instance, argue that sustainable development models are quite difficult to apply when it comes to cultural heritage since it is a non-renewable resource. On this note, I have pointed out the dearth of literature that aims at investigating the validity of Kiriama *et al*'s assertion. In view of this realisation and the main objective of this book, the present study has gone a step further to ethnographically investigate Kiriama *et al*'s assertion by assessing the extent to which cultural heritage, and in particular the BCM, has and continue to contribute to socio-economic development of local communities.

The ethnographic approach used in gathering data for this thesis made it easier for the researcher to find out what is actually prevailing on the ground to the local communities surrounding BCM site. Although I was resident in my field site for a shorter period (one month) as opposed to the tradition in anthropology as pioneered by the likes of Bronislaw Malinowski and Clifford Geertz who respectively spent several years in the Trobriand Islands and two and half years in Java studying local communities, interestingly, my study is reflective of good anthropological fieldwork with valid results. In this view, this work deconstructs the orthodox notions of fieldwork in anthropology as long drawn periods of immersion in the culture of the 'other' or participant observation as a long period of residence in the study area and as the most authentic anthropological fieldwork in Africa.

It was through observations, interviews, group focus discussions, listening to people's stories, and questionnaires that I realised that cultural heritage is to a larger extent contributing to socio-economic development of local communities surrounding the site. Though differences were observed and noted in some cases, the data gathered during fieldwork reflects that most of the information from both locals and professionals working at the site generally agree that cultural heritage sites if properly used could act as ambassadors of cultural identity and vehicles of socio-economic development. This corroborates Patrice Meyer-Bisch's (2008) observation that while cultural diversity used to be considered as an obstacle to development, democracy, modernity, and respect for human rights, it is now rightly understood as an essential resource and means for achieving them. This is to say that while culture used to assume a backseat position in issues related to politics and socio-economic development, it has emerged as a dominant force in the matrix of socio-economic development of communities around the world.

The study has also examined the participation of community members on the understanding that participation is the key driver to empowerment and sustainable development of the communities. While most of the people in rural communities cherish good relationships and interactions with cultural heritage sites, it was noted in this book that community leaders such as chiefs and elders give much importance to social benefits to do with culture and ownership.

Moreover, the study has shown the different ways local community communities the BCM have benefited (and continue to do so) through their active participation at and interaction with the site. In so doing, the study has demonstrated how other communities with similar resources could benefit themselves through their interaction with such sites. More specifically, this study has noted that benefits which the society derive from the BCM include but not limited to education, economic, cultural, entertainment, environmental, and employment creation.

Yet, not only the positive effects and contribution of the BCM were emphasised. Gender imbalance in direct employment at the sites, for example, was cited as factor that could possibly promote unsustainable livelihoods and development in local communities such as those around the site. Cultural decadence resulting mainly from drug peddling and commercial sex industry that are alleged to be slowly finding their way in Binga were also cited as unintended [negative] effects of the BCM. Besides, the study also revealed that the community has been partially excluded when it comes to management of the BCM cultural heritage site. In the light of all this, one could argue that the study manages to ensure that the objectives of the study were fulfilled and satisfied.

However, despite inadequacy of community involvement noted by some participants, the study concluded that cultural heritage can lead to socio-economic empowerment and sustainable development of the local communities if properly utilised. The local communities around the BCM, for example, have socio-economically developed despite claims by some of them that they are not involved in the management of the site. Thus, the BCM generally portrays the potential of cultural heritage to foster socio-economic status of the communities who live around heritage sites by raising their standards of life and rescue them from the effects of abject poverty.

References

Adichie, C. 2009. 'The danger of a single story,' TED Talks, Available at: http://www.ted.com.

Adorno, T. W. 1978. On the social situation of music, *Telos 35* (Spring): 129-165.

Adorno, T. W. 1982. "On the fetish character of music and the regression of hearing," In: Arato, A. and Gebhardt, E. 1982. *The essential Frankfurt School Reader*, Continuum: New York, pp. 270-299.

Adorno, T. W. 1983. 'Valery Proust Museum', in T. W. Adorno *Prisms* (trans. Samuel and Shierry Weber), pp. 175–85 Cambridge, MA: MIT Press.

Adorno, T. W. 1991. *The culture industry*, Routledge: London.

Alsop, G. and Tompsett, C. 2007. From effect to effectiveness: The missing research questions, *Educational Technology and Society*, 10 (1): 28-39.

Altieri, M. A. 1995. *Agroecology: The science of sustainable agriculture*, 2nd Edition. London: IT Publications.

Anderson, L. 2006. *Post-Conflict Security Sector Reform and the Challenge of Ownership – The Case of Liberia*, Copenhagen: Danish Institute for International Studies.

Appadurai, A. (Ed.). 1986. 'Introduction: Commodities and the Politics of Value,' In *The Social Life of Things: Commodities in Cultural Perspective*, edited by Arjun Appadurai, Cambridge University Press: Cambridge.

Barillet, C., Joffroy, T. and Longuet, I. 2006. (Eds.) *A guide for African Local Governments, Cultural Heritage and local government*, CRATerre, ENSAG/Convention France UNESCO.

BBC News, 2006. 'Carrier worries for minority women,' *BBC News*, 6 Sept 2006.

Bebbington, A. 1999. Capitals and capabilities: A framework for analysing peasant viability, rural livelihoods and poverty, *World Development* 27: 2012-44.

Benjamin, W. 1969. *Illuminations*, Shocken Publishers: New York.

Bernard, H. R. 1995. *Research methods in Anthropology*, London: Alta Mira Press.

Berthelot, J.-M. 1995. The body as a discursive operator, or, The Aporias of a sociology of the body, *Body and Society*, 1 (1): 13–23.

Breen, C. 2007. 'Advocacy, international development and World Heritage Sites in Sub-Saharan Africa in World Archaeology, Vol. 39, Number 3, *The Archaeology of World Heritage*, p.355-370, Taylor and Francis Ltd.

Byers, B. A., R. N. Cunliffe, and Hudak, A. T. 2001. "Linking the Conservation of Culture and Nature: A Case Study of Sacred Forests in Zimbabwe." *Human Ecology* 29 (2): 187–218.

Campbell, M. B. and Luckert, K. M. (Eds.) 2002. *Uncovering the hidden harvest: Valuation methods for woodland and forest resources*, Earthscan Publications Limited: London.

Carney, D. 1998. *Sustainable rural livelihoods: What contribution can we make?* Department for International Development: London.

Catholic Commission for Justice and Peace (CCJPZ). 1999. 'Breaking the silence: Building true peace,' *A Report on the Disturbances in Matabeleland and the Midlands 1980-1988*, Legal Resource Foundation: Harare.

Chabata, M. F. and Chiwaura, H. 2014. 'Memory, space and contestations in living traditions: The case of Chitungwiza chaChaminuka Shrine in Zimbabwe,' In: Mawere, M. and Mubaya, T. (Eds). *African cultures, memory and space: Living the past presence in Zimbabwean heritage*, Langaa RPCIG: Bamenda.

Chauke, C. 2003. *Community participation in management of Zimbabwe heritage sites*, Masters Thesis: University of Zimbabwe.

Chirikure, S., Manyanga, M., Ndoro, W., Pwiti, G. 2010. Unfulfilled promises: Community participation at some of Africa's World Heritage Sites, *International Journal of Heritage Studies* 16 (1 and 2): 30-44.

Collett, D. P. 1988. 'Research Conversation and Development,' In: UNDP and UNESCO Projects ZIM 88/028.

Collett, D. P. 1992. The archaeological heritage of Zimbabwe: A master plan for resource conservation and development, *National Museums and Monuments of Zimbabwe*: Harare.

Columbia Encyclopaedia, 2007. (6th Ed). *Kariba Dam*, Columbia, 31/07/2007.

Comaroff, J. and Comaroff, L. 2009. *Ethnicity, Inc.* University of Chicago Press: Chicago.

Comaroff, J. and Comaroff, L. 2012. Reflections on cultural identity: Ethnicity, intellectual property, and the commodification of collective being, *Joint Presentation at the Department of Anthropology, Classics and Ancient History (9 May 2012)*, University of Sydney.

Comaroff, J. and Comaroff, L. Ethnography and the historical imagination, *The International Journal of African Historical Studies*, 26 (2): 417-420.

Crewe, K. 2011. Chandler's Hotel San Marcos: The resort impact on a rural town, *Journal of Urban Design* 16 (1): 87-104.

Damm, C. 2005. Archaeology, ethnohistory, and oral traditions: Approaches to the indigenous past. *Norwegian Archaeological Review* 38 (2): 73–87.

Delmont, E. 2004. South African heritage development in the first decade of democracy, *African Arts* 34 (4): 39–94.

Devisch, R. and Nyamnjoh, F. (Eds). 2011. *The postcolonial turn: Re-imagining anthropology and Africa*, Langaa Research and Publishing Common Initiative Group, Bamenda: Cameroon.

Eboreime, J. 2009. 'Challenges of heritage in Africa', In: Ndoro, W., Mumma, A. and Abungu, G. (Eds.) *Cultural Heritage and the Law, Protecting Immovable heritage in English speaking countries of Sub-Saharan Africa*, Ugo Quintily S.P.A: Rome.

Fairbanks, S.J. 2010. Environmental goodness and the challenge of American culture, *Ethics and the Environment* 15 (2): 79-102.

Fairclough, N. 1989. *Language and power*, London and New York, Longman.

Faulkner, B. (Ed.) 2001. *Tourism in the twenty-first century: Reflections on experience*, Continuum Publishers: London.

Ferguson, J. T. 1996. Native Americans and the practice of archaeology, *Annual Review of Anthropology* 25: 63–79.

Fisher, J. L. 2010. *Pioneers, settlers, and aliens, exiles: The decolonisation of white identity in Zimbabwe*, Australian National University Press: Canberra.

Fontein, J. 2006. *The silence of Great Zimbabwe: Contested landscapes and the power of heritage*, Weaver Press: Harare.

Gadamer, H. G. 1987. The problem of historical consciousness, in: P. Rabinow and W.M. Sullivan, eds. *Interpretive social science: A second look*, Berkeley: University of California Press, pp. 82-140.

Garlake, P. 1975. *Great Zimbabwe*, Thames and Hudson: London.

Garlake, P. 1982. *Great Zimbabwe described and explained*, Gweru: Mambo Press.

Geertz, C. 1983. 'From the native's point of view': On the nature of anthropological understanding, In: his *Local knowledge: Further Essays in Interpretive Anthropology*, New York, 3-16.

Gell, A. 1998. *Art and Agency: Towards a New Anthropological Theory*, Clarendon Press: Oxford.

Greffe, X. 2004. Is heritage an asset or a liability? *Journal of Cultural Heritage* Vol 5 pp. 301-309, Paris.

Greffe, X. 2005. 'The future of heritage restoration businesses in Europe,' *White paper prepared for the Association of European Restoration Company*, presented on 4 October 2005.

Grever, M. De Bruijn, P. and Van Boxtel, C. 2012. Negotiating historical distance: Or how to deal with the past as a foreign country in heritage education, in: *Paedagogica Historica*, Volume 46, Number 6, pp. 878.

Halloran, J. D. 1964. *The effects of mass communication*, Leicester University Press: Leicester.

Hammar, A. 2005. Disrupting Democracy? Altering Landscapes of Local Government in Post-2000 Zimbabwe, *Discussion paper No.19. London School of Economics*, Crisis States Development Research Centre.

Harrison, P. A. M. *et al.* 2010. Identifying and prioritising services in European terrestrial and freshwater ecosystems, *Biodiversity and conservation*, 19: 2791-2821.

Heath, R. E. 2011. A theory of social agentivity and its integration into the descriptive ontology for linguistic and cognitive engineering, *International Journal on Semantic Web and Information Systems* 7 (4): 62-86.

Jackson, M. 2005. *Existential anthropology: Events, exigencies and effects*, Berghahn Books: Oxford.

Johnson, N. C. 1999. Framing the past: Time, space and the politics of heritage tourism in Ireland, in: *Political Geography*, Volume 18, pp.187–207.

Kellner, D. (n.d). *The Frankfurt School and British Cultural Studies: The missed articulation*, Illuminations: The Critical Theory Project: UCLA. Available at: http://www.gseis.ucla.edu/faculty/kellner/kellner.html.

Kendon, A. 1990.*Conducting interaction: Patterns of behaviour in focused encounters*, Cambridge University Press: Cambridge.

Kiriama, H. O.*et al.* 2010. 'Impact assessment and heritage management in Africa: Overview,' *Cultural Heritage Impact Assessment in Africa-Centre for Heritage Development in Africa*, Mombasa, Kenya.

Kopytoff, I. 1982. Slavery, *Annual Review of Anthropology*, 11: 207-30.

Kopytoff, I. 1986. 'The cultural biography of things: Commoditisation as process,' In: Appadurai, A. *The social life of things: Commodities in cultural perspectives*, Cambridge University Press: Cambridge, pp. 64- 79.

Kopytoff, I. and Miers, S. 1977. 'African "slavery" as an institution of marginality,' In: Miers, S. and Kopytoff, I. (Eds). *Slavery in Africa: Historical and anthropological perspectives*, Wisconsin: Madison, pp. 3-81.

Kuechler, S. 1987. Malangan: art and memory in a Melanesian society, *Man (N.S.)*, 22(2): 238-55.

Kuper, A. 2003. The return of the native, *Current Anthropology* 44:389–402.

Kwekudee, 2014. 'Tonga (BaTonga) people: Africa's riverine people,' Trip down memory lane, Available: at: kwekudee-tripdownmemorylane.blogspot.com, Retrieved: 25/09/2015.

Last, M. 2000. 'Reconciliation and Memory in Postwar Nigeria', In: V. Das, Arthur Kleinman, Mamphela Ramphele and Pamela Reynolds (eds) *Violence and Subjectivity*, pp. 315–32. Los Angeles: University of California Press.

Latour, B. 1993.*We have never been modern*, Cambridge, Mass: Harvard University Press.

Latour, B. 2007. The recall of modernity, *Cultural Studies Review* 13 (1): 11-30.

Lewis, M. A. and Lockheed, M. E. 2006. *Inexcusable Absence: Why 60 million girls aren't in school and what to do about it,* Center for Global Development: Washington DC.

Lien, M. and Law, J. 2010. *Emergent aliens performing indigeneity and other ways of doing salmon in Norway,* The Open University: UK.

Lowenthal, D. 1996. *Possessed by the past: The heritage crusade and the spoils of history,* New York: The Free Press.

Lowenthal, D. 1998. *The heritage crusade and the spoils of history,* Cambridge: Cambridge

Makambe, E. P. 1990. *Marginalising the human rights campaign: The dissident factor and the politics of violence in Zimbabwe, 1980-1987,* Institute of Southern African Studies, National University of Lesotho.

Makumbe, J. 1998. *Democracy and Development in Zimbabwe: Constraints of Decentralisation.* SAPES Trust: Harare.

Marshall, Y. 2002. What is community archaeology? *World Archaeology* 34:211–19.

Matenga, E. 1998. *The soapstone birds of Great Zimbabwe: Symbols of a nation,* Africa Publishing Group: Harare.

Mauss, M. 1950. "Les techniques du corps." In Sociologie et anthropologie, 365–386. Paris: PUF (Presses Universitaires de France) (first published in 1936, Journal de psychologie, XXXII, 3–4).

Mawere, M. 2013. *Environment and natural resource conservation and management in Mozambique*, Langaa Publishers: Bamenda.

Mawere, M. 2014. *Divining the future of Africa: Healing the wounds, restoring dignity and fostering development*, Langaa Research Publishing CIG: Mankon, Bamenda.

Mawere, M. 2015. *Humans, Other Beings and the Environment: Harurwa (edible stinkbugs) and Environmental Conservation in South-eastern Zimbabwe*, Cambridge University Press: Cambridge.

Mawere, M. *et al.* 2012. Convergence of diverse religions at Zimbabwe heritage sites: The case of Great Zimbabwe National Monument, *International Research Journal of Arts and Social Sciences,* Vol. 1 (2): 22-31.

McManamon, F. 2000. Archaeological messages and messengers, *Public Archaeology* 1:5–20.

McQuail, D. 'The influence and effects of mass media,' In: Curran, J. et al. 1979. (Eds). *Mass communication and society*, Sage Publications, Berverly Hills, pp. 1-23.

Meinzen-Dick, R., and R. Pradhan. 2002. "Legal Pluralism and Dynamic Property Rights," CAPRI Working Paper no 22. CGIAR System-wide Programme on Collective Action and Property Rights. Washington DC.

Meyer-Bisch, P. 2008. 'Defining the value of cultural rights and diversity,' In: Nowicki, J., Oustinoff, M. and Proulx, S. (Eds). *The challenge of culture, no. 51.* Institut des Sciences de la Communication, Sorbonne: Paris.

Moscardo, G. 2001. 'Cultural and heritage tourism: The great debate,' In: Faulkner, B. (Ed.) *Tourism in the twenty-first century: Reflections on experience*, Continuum Publishers: London.

Mowforth, M. and Munt, I. 2003. *Tourism and Sustainability: Development and New Tourism in the Third World*, Routledge: London.

Moyo, S. 2000. (Ed). *Zimbabwe environmental dilemma: Balancing resource inequalities*, Zimbabwe Environmental Research Organisation: Harare.

Munikwa, C. 2011. *The Binga Outreach: The Contextualisation of Mission in the Reformed Church in Zimbabwe*, Dissertation Presented for the Degree of Doctor of Theology in the Faculty of Theology, Stellenbosch University, South Africa.

Muzvidziwa, V. 2004. Reflections on ethical issues: A study of how urban women dealt with impoverishment, Nordic Journal of African Studies, 13 (3): 302-318.

Ncube, G. T. 2004. *A History of North Western Zimbabwe 1850-1960*, Mond Books: Kadoma.

Ndoro, W. 2001a. *The Preservation of Great Zimbabwe: Your monument our shrine*, Department of Archaeology and Ancient History, Uppsala University: Uppsala.

Ndoro, W. 2005. The Preservation of Great Zimbabwe: *Your monument our shrine*, Rome: ICCROM.

Ndoro, W. 2001b. Heritage management in Africa, *Conservation, The Getty Conservation Institute Newsletter*, Volume 16 (3):1-7.

Nurse, K. 2006. 'Culture as the fourth pillar of sustainable development,' *Paper prepared for Commonwealth Secretariat*, Paris, UNESCO 2000: 30-34.

Nyamnjoh, F. B. 2012. Blinded by sight: Divining the future of anthropology in Africa, *Africa Spectrum*, 47 (2-3): 63-92.

Pearce, D. W. and Atkinson, G. D. 1993. 'Capital theory and the measurement of sustainable development: an indicator of "weak" sustainability,' *Ecological Economics* 8: 103-108.

Pwiti, G. 1996. Let the ancestors rest in peace? New challenges for cultural heritage management in Zimbabwe, *Conservation and Management of Archaeological Sites* 1:151–60.

Pwiti, G. and Chirikure, S. 2008. Community involvement in archaeology and cultural heritage management – An assessment from case studies in Southern Africa and elsewhere, *Journal of Current Anthropology*, Vol. 49, Number 3.

Pwiti, G. and Mvenge, G. 1996. Archaeologists, tourists and rainmakers: problems in the management of rock art sites in Zimbabwe: a case study of Domboshava National Monument, In: Pwiti, G. & Soper R. (Eds.). *Aspects of African Archaeology*, Harare, University of Zimbabwe, 817-24.

94

Ranger, T. O. 1999. *Voices from the rocks: Nature, culture and history in the Matopo hills*, Baobab: Harare.

Reynolds, P. and Cousins, T. 1989. *Lwaano lwanyika: Tonga book of the earth*, Baobab Books: Harare.

Ross, F. 2005. Codes and dignity: Thinking about ethics in relation to research on violence. *Anthropology Southern Africa*, 2005, 28 (3 and 4): 99-107.

Rossler, M. and Saouma-Forero, G. 1999. The World Heritage Convention and Cultural Landscapes in Africa. Paris, UNESCO.

Rowlands, M. 1985. Notes on the material symbolism of grassfields palaces, Paideuma Bd. 31, In: *Palaces and chiefly households in the Cameroon grassfields*, Frobenius Institute Stable: Frankfurt, pp. 203-213.

Rowlands, M. 1993.The role of memory in the transmission of a culture, *World Archaeology*, 25 (2): 141-151.

Rowlands, M. 2008. Civilisation, violence, and heritage healing in Liberia, *Journal of Material Culture*, 13 (2): 135-152.

Rowley, S. 2002. Inuit participation in the archaeology of Nunavut: A historical overview. In *Honouring our elders, a history of Eastern Arctic archaeology*, ed. W. Fitzhugh, S. Loring, and D. Odess, 261–72, Smithsonian Institution: Washington DC.

Rukuni, J. & Eicher, C. K. 1994. *Zimbabwe's agricultural revolution*, University of Zimbabwe Publications: Harare.

Rypkema, D. 2009. 'Economics and the built cultural heritage' In: Therond, D. and Trigona, A. (eds.) *Heritage and Beyond*, Council of Europe Publishing: Europe.

Sagiya, M., Mubaya T. R. and Mawere, M. 2013. Challenges, Dilemmas and Potentialities for Poverty Relief by Heritage Sites in Zimbabwe: Voices from Chibvumani Heritage site Stakeholders, *Journal of Sustainable Development in Africa*, 15 (1): 186- 198.

Salpeteur, M. and Warnier, J- P. 2013. Looking for the effects of bodily organs and substances through vernacular public autopsy in Cameroon, *Critical African Studies* 5 (3): 153–174.

Schilder, P. 1964. *The Image and Appearance of the Human Body: Studies in the Constructive Energy of the Psyche*, London: Kegan Paul.

Scoones, I. and F. Matose. 1993. Local Woodland Management: Constraints and Opportunities for Sustainable Resource Management, In: *Living with Trees: Policies for Forestry Management in Zimbabwe*, edited by P. N. Bradley, and K. McNamara, 157–93. Washington DC: The World Bank.

Seixas, P. F. 2014. History and heritage: What is the difference? In: *Canadian Issues*, pp.12-17.

Sen, A. 1990. 'Development as capability expansion', In: Griffin, Keith and Knight, John (eds.). *Human Development and the International Development Strategy for the 1990s*, London: Macmillan, pp. 41-58.

Shklovsky, V. 1917. (Cited in Crawford, L.1984). Viktor Shklovsky: Difference in defamiliarisation, *Comparative Literature*, 36 (3): 209-219.

Silberberg, T. 1995. Cultural tourism and business opportunity for museums and heritage sites, *Tourism Management,* 16 (5): 361-65.

Silver, H. 1994. Social Exclusion and Social Solidarity, *International Labour Review 133*, nos. 5-6 (1994): 531-78.

Tanselle, T. 1998. *Literature and artifacts*, Bibliographical Society of the University of Virginia: Charlottesville.

Taruvinga, P. and Ndoro, W. 2003. The vandalism of the Domboshava rock painting site, Zimbabwe: Some reflections on approaches to heritage management, *Conservation and Management of Archaeological Sites* 6 (1): 3-10.

Teffo, J. 1994. *Towards a conceptualization of Ubuntu*, Pretoria: Ubuntu School of Philosophy.

Tejaswi, S. 26 May 2011. 'What is the relationship between history and heritage?' downloaded from www.preservearticles.com, Accessed 10 October 2015.

Thondhlana, T. 2015. 'Old wine in new bottles': A critical historiographical survey of Zimbabwean museum institutions': In: Mawere, M. *et al.* (Eds). *African museums in the making: Reflections on the politics of material and public culture in Zimbabwe*, Langaa Publishers: Cameroon.

Timothy, D. J. and Nyaupane, G. P. 2009. *Cultural heritage and tourism in the developing world: A regional perspective*, Routledge: London.

University Press.

Van Binsbergen, W. M. J. 2003. *Intercultural encounters: African and anthropological lessons towards a philosophy of interculturality*, Lit Verlag, Munster.

Verran, H. 2011. Engagements between disparate knowledge traditions: Towards doing difference generatively and in good faith, *A paper presented to Contested Ecologies conference*, Mont Flaer: Cape Town.

Von Uexkull, J. *A foray into the worlds of animals and humans, with a theory of meaning*, (trans. Joseph, D. O'Neil), 2010. University of Minnesota Press: Minnesota.

Warnier, J. -P. 2005. 'Inside and outside: Surfaces and containers,' Tilley, pp. 186-196.

Warnier, J.-P. 2001. A praxeological approach to subjectivation in a material world, *Journal of Material Culture*, 6 (1): 5–24.

Warnier, J.-P. 2007. *The Pot-King: The Body and Technologies of Power*, Boston, MA: Brill.

Watkins, J. 2003. Beyond the margin: American Indians, First Nations, and anthropology in North America, *American Antiquity* 68:273–85.

World Commission on Dams, 2000. *Kariba Dam, Zambia and Zimbabwe*, Final Report, World Commission on Dams.

World Commission on Environment and Development, 1987. *Our Common Future*, (Brundtland Report), Oxford University Press: Oxford.

Zimbabwe National Culture Policy, 2015. *The Zimbabwe National Culture Policy Draft*, Ministry of Sport, Arts, and Culture, Harare: Zimbabwe.

Printed in the United States
By Bookmasters